Dewees
The Island and Its People

James Cochrane

Charleston ~ London

History
PRESS

Published by The History Press
Charleston, SC 29403
www.historypress.net

Copyright © 2007 by James Cochrane
All rights reserved

Cover art: Painting by Margaret Hilton. Photograph of beach by Judy Fairchild. Photograph of marsh by Wharton Winstead. Dewees Island, South Carolina.

First published 2007

Manufactured in the United Kingdom

ISBN 978.1.59629.339.7

Library of Congress CIP data applied for.

In memory of Deedee Paschal, whose vision comprehended the South Carolina barrier islands as an irreplaceable natural treasure, and whose determination inspired creation of the Deedee Paschal Barrier Island Trust to understand the islands, and through understanding, to preserve them.

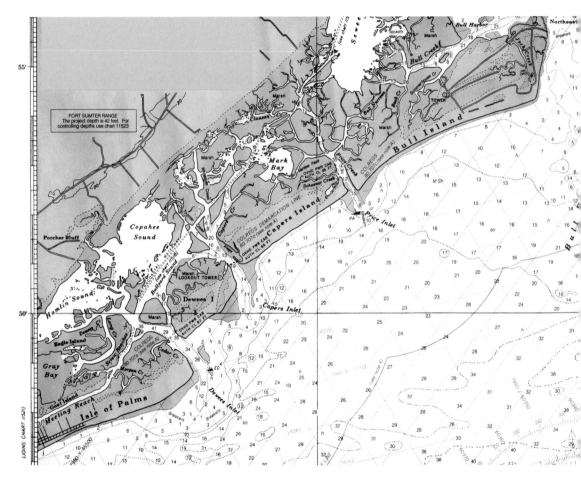

Map of Dewees Island and vicinity. *National Oceanic and Atmospheric Administration.*

Contents

Acknowledgements

J ohn Knott, developer of Dewees Island, maintains that Dewees is a community made up of people who share a common love of this beautiful environment, common experience and common interest. Community support has been apparent at every step of my writing, and I thank all who have contributed. My thanks begin with the photographers who have permitted me to use their work. I am also grateful to the artists who have allowed the use of photographic images of their paintings, and to the present owners of these paintings.

I was appointed a member of the Dewees Archives Committee after moving to the island in 2000, and within the next six months I began e-mail correspondence with Edgar Taylor, a descendant of the Dewees family; a correspondence that still continues. I thank Ed for the abundant family information and interesting speculations he has sent. I also thank Nina and Don Reynolds (with whom, unfortunately, I have lost touch) for sending newsletters of the Dewees/Deweese Family Association. Without their help, valuable Dewees family information would have been unavailable. E-mail correspondence with Eddie Collins brought information regarding his great-grandfather, John D. Murphy, an owner of the island around 1898.

Jack Huyler first came to Dewees Island in 1924 as a four-year-old. On several occasions he has returned to the island and has given to Dewees Island photographs of island life and scenes during the years the Huyler family were the owners. It is gratifying that Jack continues to hold fond memories of Dewees. I appreciate his contributions.

Conversations with former owners and management have been rewarding. I appreciated talking with R.S. Reynolds III concerning his family's ownership of Dewees Island, and with Oscar Leppert, the island caretaker during those years, and his sons, Larry and Mark. Their recollections have helped me to better understand life on Dewees between 1956 and 1972. I have had rewarding conversations with Ed Royall on the Seewed experience, and with John Knott regarding the Island Preservation Partnership. My further thanks to Ed Royall for his personal files for the years 1972–1990, and for reading a draft of the book's coverage of those years. I have benefited from Leslie

Sautter's knowledge of Dewees Island geology and Karl Ohlandt's knowledge of plants and animals. Elizabeth Williamson read the entire manuscript, and I thank her for her contribution. Joe Sommerich read a draft of the entire history, for which I am grateful.

I thank all the Dewees Community who have been interested in the book's progress. My appreciation goes to the librarians at the Charleston County Public Library and the Charleston Library Society. Their help and their collections of South Carolina books allowed me to do nearly all my research without leaving Charleston. I also thank Lee Handford and others at The History Press for their interest, and for guiding this first-time author through the publishing process.

Very special thanks are given to three wonderful colleagues. I had not met Linda Dayhoff Smith before the spring of 2007, when she sent an e-mail noting that she had seen on the Dewees Island website a reference to my book and offering information regarding her family members who had lived on Dewees Island a century or more ago. Using original documents filed at the South Carolina Department of Archives and History, she has traced the lives of numerous Dewees owners, unearthing fascinating details about everyday life on Dewees in the eighteenth and nineteenth centuries. Linda has also read the book chapters that drew on her research.

The History Press guide to authors provides detailed specifications for photographic images. All must be scanned at 300dpi, and saved with the extension of TIFF. These directions, meant to be helpful, were beyond my comprehension, let alone execution. Fortunately, Wharton Winstead, an outstanding photographer himself, scanned photographs taken between 1900 and 2007 by photographers of varying experience and ability. His work met or exceeded the publisher's requirements. Wharton has my grateful appreciation.

My wife, Jill, has stored on her computer all of my vaguely legible manuscript and has suggested dozens of improvements. She has collected and arranged the individual photographs and CDs that were loaned. Jill also assembled a bibliography, and has encouraged me whenever the project seemed to drag.

The contributions of Jill, Wharton and Linda merit all the gratitude I express and more.

Chapter 1

A Place Apart

The coast of South Carolina is fringed by a series of low islands, or sandbars, on the exterior lines of which the receding tide leaves exposed broad beaches formed by gradually shelving shores. These islands are covered with glistening white sands, forming little hills, which shift with the varying winds. At the time of the Revolution they were covered with palmettos and myrtle with here and there a live-oak or a cedar tree…On the interior side of these islands are immense tracts of green salt marsh, extending for miles between the islands and the mainland. These marshes are intersected by labyrinths of narrow serpentine creeks through which the flooding water makes its tortuous way, and often at the spring-tide overflows them, completely obliterating for the time the creeks through which it has come from the sea. At low water these creeks are usually bare.
—*Edward McCrady, A History of South Carolina in the Revolution, 1901*

This passage describes the South Carolina sea islands at the time of the American Revolution. It also portrays the barrier islands as they appeared for countless earlier centuries. Although South Carolina Native Americans had used the islands for hunting and fishing, island villages were few and small, and the islands were little affected. Difficulties of travel between the islands and the mainland, and severity of storms on the exposed coast discouraged settlement. Plantations existed on several of the islands before the Revolution, but they were designed and built to harmonize with the natural environment. While rice culture destroyed thousands of acres of mainland marsh and forest, the islands were generally poorly suited for rice planting and island marshes remained undisturbed. Island environment was little affected by the small farms that adjoined plantation houses.

More extensive settlement began on some of the South Carolina islands in the years following the Revolution. The city of Charleston and the rice plantations of the coastal rivers were known to be unhealthy during the summer months. Prosperous planters and city dwellers found nearby island air more healthful and built vacation homes close to the ocean. Fort Moultrie, constructed on Sullivan's Island immediately before the Revolution, continued to be an army base, and the South Carolina legislature authorized rental of land for residential construction in the vicinity of the fort. Hurricane winds and storm surges destroyed homes and caused frequent loss of life, but Sullivan's Island continued to attract summer residents throughout the early years of the nineteenth century. The community of Secessionville on James Island (so named because its residents had seceded from the mosquito-infested plantations) and Edingsville on Edisto Island were established in the first half of the nineteenth century. Other small communities were created on St. Helena's and Hilton Head Islands. Farther north, planters built cottages for summer occupancy on North and South Islands, while Pawley's Island had a cluster of beach cottages by 1840.

These efforts at island development ended with the Civil War. Men were called to arms, and their wives and children were removed to safer areas. Labor for cultivation was difficult to obtain. Fugitives and escaped slaves found refuge on the abandoned farms. The creeks and inlets bordering the islands were used by blockade runners while Union vessels patrolled the coast and landed forces of occupation.

The end of the war did not bring any revival of island settlement. Few South Carolinians were able to rebuild and maintain their homes, titles to land were in dispute and disastrous hurricanes swept away houses on islands bordering the coast. The Edisto Island village of Edingsville was destroyed in 1883 by a storm that brought a fifteen-foot surge. Poverty and natural disasters seemed likely to return the coastal islands to wilderness.

At the very end of the nineteenth century, Joseph S. Lawrence, a forerunner of the island developers to come, conceived the idea of opening Long Island to recreation use. Fort Moultrie was still an army post, while small villages existed on Sullivan's Island and in Mount Pleasant. In 1898 Lawrence built a trolley line beginning in Mount Pleasant, crossing a bridge to Sullivan's Island and then passing over Breach Inlet to Long Island, which he renamed Isle of Palms. A pier and pavilion were built on Isle of Palms, and an amusement center with a Ferris wheel attracted visitors from Charleston as well as from Moultrieville and Mount Pleasant. Land sales, however, did not follow. Isle of Palms was too isolated, overgrown and snake infested to attract residents.

A few years later a new road across James Island attracted a small number of residents to Folly Island. The beach at Folly Island has been described as a tent city, but derelict boxcars as well as tents constituted most of the community buildings. For Folly Beach and Isle of Palms, as well as other coastal islands, development was to be a product of the mid-twentieth century.

Improvements in transportation that would advance residential development of South Carolina's islands materialized in the years following World War I. Construction of an intracoastal waterway from Virginia to Florida had been contemplated for years, and during the 1930s creeks separating the South Carolina islands from the mainland were deepened and straightened. In 1940, construction of the Atlantic Intracoastal Waterway was complete, and its maintenance was assumed by the Army Corps of Engineers. Pleasure cruisers and sailboats as well as commercial craft could travel from island to island along the coast.

Far more significant for the islands' future was the construction of bridges and improvement of highways. The Coastal Highway (now U.S. 17) had long been the principal north–south route along the coast. President George Washington followed this road on his trip to South Carolina in 1791, but it remained only a track through the forest throughout the nineteenth century. A traveler from Charleston to Georgetown had to cross four rivers by ferry between the Cooper and the Santee. In the 1920s bridges were erected across these rivers, and by 1930 South Carolina's Coastal Highway was straightened and paved. The age of the automobile had arrived and the new highways invited the traveler to the coast. Bridges to many of the islands were in place, and the beauty of the still undeveloped islands attracted the modern settler.

Economic and political factors postponed the immediate settlement of the islands. During the Depression of the 1930s Americans were little able to purchase land or build cottages for a new or vacation home. The coming of total war in 1941 limited use of the family automobile. Only the return to peace and a new prosperity in the next decade brought the islands to the attention of developers.

Hilton Head Island was the site for the first and largest postwar development in South Carolina. First settled in the 1720s, Hilton Head Island produced indigo and subsequently, long staple cotton. The island climate was unhealthy and few planters lived there. After the Civil War, wealthy Northerners acquired most of the plantation lands and used them as private game preserves. In 1949 investors in timberland purchased twenty thousand acres of pine forest and founded the Hilton Head Company. Its manager, Charles E. Fraser, foresaw Hilton Head Island's potential as a resort community and in 1956 began the sale of land in Sea Pines Plantation. The first beach lots were sold in 1958 for a price of $5,350. Construction of championship golf courses, addition of resort hotels and stores and effective promotion of a planned development promising controlled growth and environmental protection made Hilton Head an immediate and continuing vacation and retirement success. Other plantations on the island were opened in later years attracting increasing numbers of investors and visitors. By 1995 Hilton Head Island boasted a year-round population of twenty-eight thousand with over 1.5 million visitors.

The success of Hilton Head inspired development of the smaller Seabrook and Kiawah Islands. Each had been privately owned since the late seventeenth century, and the families of the early settlers retained ownership for more than two hundred years. Seabrook Island was sold in 1951 to real estate brokers who proceeded to prepare the island for development. Sale of lots commenced in 1972. Kiawah Island was purchased by lumberman C.C. Royall in 1950 for $125,000. He logged the remaining timber and in 1974 sold his interest to investors from Kuwait for a price of $17,000,000. Both islands were effectively marketed to prospective vacationers and retirees as environmentally protected, luxurious residential communities.

North of Charleston, Isle of Palms development began earlier and progressed more slowly than on Seabrook and Kiawah. The trolley line followed by the construction of automobile bridges brought vacationers to the southern end of Isle of Palms. As late as 1940, however, only two dozen residents regarded the island as a full-time home.

Change began in 1944, when J.C. Long purchased a large part of the southern half of Isle of Palms and energetically promoted home building. In 1974, the population of Isle of Palms was almost four thousand, with summer visitors doubling it. Wild Dunes Resort with its golf courses and marina, and the development of the remainder of Isle of Palms, produced a further population growth.

In general, residential settlement of South Carolina's barrier islands had been stimulated by experienced and aggressive real estate developers. They laid out winding streets, carefully sited lots, replaced the natural undergrowth with trees and grass and set aside public areas for residents' use. They planned and offered golf and tennis, a community recreation center and hotel, restaurant and retail facilities.

Folly Island is an example of less systematically organized development. In 1918 a group of Charleston businessmen purchased a large area of the island including the beach. They laid out streets and commenced the sale of lots. Eight years later bridges were built, opening Folly Beach to automobile traffic. A pavilion and restaurants soon followed, and modest cottages replaced the tents and boxcars of earlier years. Despite storms that periodically swept away oceanfront houses, the population of Folly Island has grown steadily.

The dramatic increase in coastal island population has been accompanied by the growth of such South Carolina communities bordering the coast as Myrtle Beach, Mount Pleasant and Beaufort. A report issued by Clemson University in 2002 concluded that South Carolina coastal counties are growing much faster than the state average and attracting more retirees with larger incomes. From 1980 to 2000 the coastal county population grew by more than 43 percent, while the average of other counties increased 24 percent. Coastal South Carolina has been identified as one of the top five retirement areas in the country.

The increasing concentration of coastal residents has alarmed conservationists and planners. In the spring of 2002, Dana Beach, president of the South Carolina Coastal Council, prepared a paper for the Pew Oceans Commission expressing concern that population growth would irrevocably change the character of coastal islands and the adjoining mainland. Mayor Joseph Riley of Charleston, chairman of the Pew Commission's Coastal Development Committee, commented: "If coastal development continues at the same pace and technique, it will eventually destroy the sustainability of coastal waters."

Sustainability, a word omitted from some dictionaries a generation ago, is now a key term for planners and forecasters. The word, of course, comes from "sustain" and refers to the capacity of an organism, a species, a community or a culture to "hang in there," to survive and keep going despite adversities or changed conditions. South Carolina's barrier islands have overcome demanding environmental tests: violent winds, tidal surges, wildfires, droughts and disease. The islands are examples of natural sustainability. This quality is apparent in recovery from hurricanes.

It is the physical composition of coastal barrier islands that enables them to survive hurricanes and provide some protection to the mainland behind them. A barrier island is typically made up of three components: the beach including its dunes, the maritime forest and the salt marsh. Freshwater wetlands may also be present in the island's interior. Each part of the island may establish defenses, which help protect the whole island. For example, a wide beach, particularly a beach with abundant dunes and vegetation, reduces the risk that storm waves will break through the beach and penetrate inland. Vegetation growing on and about the dunes may hold the sand in place, helping the dune maintain integrity against waves. The higher, wider and more continuous the dune system, the greater its protection. Studies in the aftermath of Hurricane Hugo in 1989 concluded that natural dunes proved to be the most effective surge barrier.

Dunes do not materially obstruct high winds, but forest cover is effective in reducing wind damage. Broad salt marshes and wetlands take up storm surge, helping to protect inland areas. An acre of wetland, flooded to a depth of a foot, holds approximately 330,000 gallons of water that would otherwise cover the forest floor. Thus, all of the natural island works together to reduce coastal storm effects.

An undisturbed environment also aids an island's recovery from storm damage. Forest destruction during Hurricane Hugo was extensive. Between 85 and 90 percent of mature pines in the storm-centered area of Francis Marion National Forest were destroyed, together with nearly every mature pine on the nearby sea islands. Within a few years new, young trees were growing, and the forests were noticeably regaining their vegetation. The most lasting damage came from heavy equipment used in the clean up, and from huge fires used to burn fallen trees.

Storm surges of sixteen feet and more during Hugo covered the islands between Charleston and Cape Romain, without permanent damage to the soil and vegetation of the marsh. Dunes were swept away, but their reformation began almost immediately. Debris from the storm collected and sheltered sand, and small beach plants quickly found a place to grow. Some beaches actually widened as offshore sandbars deposited by the storm migrated onshore. Storm-generated inlets in the beach created by surf overwash gradually filled in and closed naturally.

While a barrier island maintains sustainability despite natural disasters, it does not fare well when exposed to unwise development. Human actions may change the shoreline, introduce pollutants to the water and soil and destroy the island's natural resources. The coastal developers and those to whom they sold land and houses did not set out or desire to impair the islands' sustainability. Developers promoted and praised the ocean, the beaches, the green marshes, the meandering creeks and the tranquility of the islands. These were natural features that were expected to—and did—attract residents. But the developers also wished to offer more—waterfront living, paved roads for automobiles and paved walkways to afford easy beach access, lush lawns and golf courses and docks for boat mooring. Purchasers and builders welcomed these amenities, which have been important considerations in the dynamic population growth along South Carolina's coast. The additional attractions, going beyond the natural beauty the islands offer, have been instrumental in threatening the coastal present and future, for it has become evident that the effort to make the island a man-made luxury attraction is incompatible with the inherent nature of the islands.

The clearest demonstration of this incompatibility has been the construction of waterfront houses. Proximity to the ocean is the dominant reason to live on an ocean island. Vacationers wanted houses directly on the beach. To hear the surf and to walk out the door onto the edge of the ocean was the essence of island living. Building directly on or in front of the dunes assured the closest approach.

What the oceanfront resident did not comprehend was that the beach had never agreed to keep its place. Beginning with the earliest settlements on Pawley's, Sullivan's, Folly and Edisto Islands, beach homes washed into the sea as storm waves and high tides removed the sand. Loss of dunes made beach erosion more certain and destructive. Sometimes whole streets of houses disappeared. Other houses, farther from the ocean became waterfront, only to face destruction when the next intense storm passed. It might seem that a reasonable way to protect homes from erosion would be to build them back from the shore, preferably well behind the dunes. This, however, was not as appealing as attempting to force the beach to remain in place. The customary approach to beach erosion has been—and in many cases still is—to prevent waves from moving the beach by constructing a barrier that would shield it from the ocean. Beach armoring uses a variety of materials and takes many shapes. The most common materials are sandbags, rocks, concrete, metal and wood. They may be placed near a threatened building, deposited on the beach or made into a wall.

The most readily apparent objection to beach armoring is its appearance. Sandbags are an eyesore and the sight of rocks and masonry inevitably detract from the view. Artificial stabilizers on a beach lessen the pleasure of beach walking and may make swimming hazardous.

Less damage is done by replenishing sand that has been washed away, but it is acknowledged that replacing sand is only a temporary benefit. If a beach must be restored to preserve property, replenishment is generally considered preferable to artificial hardening. Much better, though, is leaving the beach and its dunes undisturbed and constructing homes well back from all coastal sand.

Other changes brought about by increasing population density have also decreased the sustainability of barrier islands. The arrival of automobiles, the paving of roads and parking areas, the removal of native ground cover, the construction of golf courses and retail stores and the filling of wetlands—all of these alter the island's environment. Further, to the extent they attract short-term renters, they discourage the creation of a true community life.

In their book *Sea Islands of the South*, Diana and Bill Gleasner summarize the natural sustainability of barrier islands and the multiple threats presented by human overdevelopment:

> *The island was apparently engineered with flexibility in mind. It can bend without breaking. Hurricane opened inlets relieve stress, sand builds up in one area, temporarily abandoning another. Enter man with plans to improve the whole thing by dredging here, building a sea wall there. He thins out the forest to build a hotel, not realizing that trees form a canopy over under growth, which is not salt-tolerant. When ocean spray attacks the ground cover, it no longer holds down the soil. This loss of vegetation allows sediment to erode, thereby dooming the remaining trees.*

What alternatives are there to overdevelopment and the sacrifice of a natural island? One approach is legislative limits on growth. South Carolina has laws that seek to prevent the damage caused by overdevelopment. Restrictions are placed on beach engineering, construction of docks, draining or infilling wetlands. But the success of legislation is limited and uncertain. The influence of real estate and development interests inhibits truly significant restriction; constitutional prohibitions against the taking of property without full compensation to the owner are raised wherever a property owner is restricted in what he may do with his land.

A more sweeping alternative is for the island owner to dedicate his land to a permanent natural condition. Some South Carolina barrier islands remain in private ownership as wildlife preserves. North Island and South Island, situated just above the Santee River delta, are part of the Tom Yawkee Wildlife Preserve. The largest area of undeveloped South Carolina islands is the Cape Romain National Wildlife Refuge. It was established by the United States in 1932, and is protected against development. Bull Island, a part of the Cape Romain Refuge, is accessible by boat and has hiking trails, but is closed to private ownership. The island immediately south of Bull Island is Capers Island, now owned by the State of South Carolina and protected under the Heritage Trust Program. On a few other islands, South Carolina state parks preserve the natural environment.

Wildlife refuges, whether government owned or created by private covenant, assist natural sustainability. By their very nature, though, they treat humans as intruders, either excluded altogether or admitted as temporary visitors. Is there no alternative? Humanity is, after all, a part of the environment. The eagerness of humans to visit and live on islands, beaches and marshes demonstrates man's affinity for nature.

In 1991 the Island Preservation Partnership (IPP), the new owner of Dewees Island, and the island's developer and chief executive, John Knott, decided that it was possible for people to live in harmony with the natural environment. Dewees, a barrier island lying between Isle of Palms and Capers Island, had been privately owned for nearly three hundred years, but it had never experienced development. Rich in seafood and wildlife, it had been used as a hunting and fishing retreat. Its wide beaches, clear inlets, broad marsh and live oak, palmetto and pine forest proclaimed its residential potential.

To protect against the consequences of unwise home construction, IPP adopted permanent protective obligations binding all purchasers of island lots. Lots were sold subject to covenants assuring that a house would not have a negative effect upon one's neighbor or on the native environment and natural characteristics of the island. No structure was permitted on the ocean beach or proximate to the dunes. Homesites were set back in the forested area between the beach and marsh. Private docks were not allowed. Marshes and natural wetlands could not be drained or filled. The size of homes and cleared area around them was limited. Native trees could only be removed if permitted by a review board. Neither lawns nor vegetation foreign to the island could be planted. Watering of trees and shrubs required reliance on cisterns that collected rainwater. Home construction was made subject to compliance with regulations issued and administered by an architectural resource board. This board insisted that residences be sited to harmonize with the island's character, that they be built with maximum use of natural, recycled or sustainable building materials and that the use of toxic or environmentally hazardous products be avoided.

Policies were also established to protect and sustain that part of the island that would be common property of all owners. The number of lots was limited to 150, leaving 65 percent of the island permanently owned in common and remaining undeveloped. No groins, seawalls or other artificial structures would be built on a beach. Island roads would be left unpaved and the only motorized vehicles permitted would be contractors' trucks and essential maintenance and emergency equipment. Boardwalks leading to the beach would cross on top of existing dunes rather than cutting through them, and access to the beach would be restricted to boardwalks. A golf course would not be built, and the community-owned buildings would meet the requirements established for residences.

Dewees Island has not been developed to appeal to every variety of resident. Its development rests on the philosophy that humans are a part of the environment, just as animals and birds, trees and undergrowth, marsh and beach are part of the environment. They can live in harmony and mutual sustainability.

Landing dock on Dewees Island. *Courtesy of Joseph McAlhany Jr.*

Chapter 2

The Face of a Barrier Island

Below McClellanville, the Waterway follows a fairly straight and not particularly interesting course chiefly through marshland, across and along innumerable creeks, rivers, sounds, bays, and inlets for 29 miles to the entrance channel to the next port, Mount Pleasant, five miles nearer than Charleston. This is one of the few parts of the Waterway which we found monotonous.
—Fessenden S. Blanchard, A Cruising Guide to the Southern Coast, 1954

The portion of the waterway that Blanchard describes as "not particularly interesting" is bordered on one side by the marshes of Mount Pleasant and on the other by the marshes of Dewees and other barrier islands. Blanchard is correct in observing that this stretch of waterway is along innumerable creeks, rivers, sounds, bays and inlets. It is a world of water and marsh, with occasional hammocks of live oak and palmetto. It is flat, the land as level as the water.

Low and flat as the water and grass are, they are far from monotonous to those living beside them. The changing color of the marsh is one of its beauties. In the winter it is dead brown. As spring comes, little patches of green appear, at first along the creeks, then spreading to the depths of the marsh. By midsummer the marsh is vivid green, and with the coming of fall the green gradually changes to gold. Highly angled light also brings out color in the marsh. When the first rays of the morning sun strike the spring and summertime grass, it has a bright yellow glitter, turning to a dark green as the day progresses. At sunset, if there has been a light cloud cover above the horizon, water in the marsh takes on the dramatic colors of the sky—red, pink and gold—while overhead shades of blue contribute to the spectacle. As the light slowly fades the marsh becomes progressively darker until all is night.

It is both the light and seasonal change that produce the varied and ever-changing color of the marsh. But twice daily the rising tide covers the grass, partially in some locations, completely in others. Vast sections of marsh, visibly covered with grass at noon, are freshly created lagoons by evening. This varied appearance of the marsh, from a meadow to a world of water, is a delight to those who see it.

The marsh observer also takes pleasure in the marsh birds and animals: the secretive marsh hen, the ducks and cormorants that gather in secluded channels, the egrets and herons standing motionless, waiting for fish that venture too close, the ospreys that search for food from high above the creeks and plunge downward with claws extended toward a moving target. Most prominent among the animals are the raccoons wading into the low water as a tide recedes. More rarely, alligators may be seen moving between marsh water and a freshwater wetland. An experienced observer finds small marine creatures, the fiddler crab and the periwinkle, their behavior fixed by the rise and fall of the tide.

Then there are the sounds of the marsh. Some of these are birdcalls, others the burbling and croaking of small marsh residents heard as the ground turns muddy at low tide. Finally, there is the silence of the marsh, especially toward evening, a silence beautiful and moving as darkness covers the water and land. It is possible to feel that you alone exist in such a soundless world.

More than half of Dewees Island is marshland. The marsh varies in width from a mile or more at its widest point, to a hundred yards or less at the north and south extremities. With the exception of occasional salt flats, grass grows in all parts of the marsh. Most of the grass is smooth cord grass (*Spartina alterniflora*).

About 70 percent of the Dewees soil lies in the marsh, a mixture of clay to silty loam. It is known as Capers series soil, perhaps in the belief that the soil originated on Capers Island. Dewees and the other "Hunting Islands" are not touched by a major river delta, but fifty miles to the north the great Santee River once poured tons of sediment into the Atlantic. Longshore currents eventually washed the sediment and organic matter south to Bull Island and beyond. Sediment deposits on Capers Island and offshore sandbars moved to Dewees and formed the natural soil of the Dewees marsh. Damming of the Santee has greatly reduced the flow of sediment, but its effect on Dewees Island has not been determined. Ultimately, however, a reduced flow will necessarily decrease the amount of sediment and sand from the north.

The interior of Dewees Island is mostly forest. Except where sandy inland roads and an occasional trail cut through the trees, the forest is dense and sometimes impenetrable. The beauty of the woods can best be observed from the roads, where overhanging trees create a green tunnel. There are animals here, but usually invisible, and even the birds are concealed among leaves. A patient watcher, though, will perceive a fluttering from branch to branch and small birds in the road and the bordering grass. Except for a few intruders that are not native to the island, the trees are the same varieties that have been here as long as written records exist: pine, oak, palmetto, cedar, magnolia and bay. Many shrubs grow beneath the trees, the wax myrtle and yaupon holly being the most common.

Sidney Lanier described the romantic beauty of maritime forest. He wrote of Glynn County, Georgia, but his words can also be used for the Dewees Island forest.

> *Glooms of the live-oaks, beautiful-braided and woven*
> *With intricate shades of the vines that myriad-cloven*
> *Clamber the forks of the multiform boughs,—*

Emerald twilights,—
   Virginal shy lights,
Wrought of the leaves to allure to the whisper of vows,
When lovers pace timidly down through the green colonnades
   Of the dim sweet woods, of the dear dark woods,
   Of the heavenly woods and glades,
That run to the radiant marginal sand-beach within
   The wide sea-marshes of Glynn;—

Turning from romance to the specifics of Dewees Island maritime forest, the woodland floor rarely rises more then fifteen feet above sea level. It is not entirely flat. Alternating ridges and swales are found in a number of the forest areas. At least some of the ridges are regarded as ancient dunes, indicating that at times in the past, beach erosion brought the ocean much farther inland than it does today. Increasing supplies of sand made possible the growth of woodland.

Four named tidal creeks connect the marsh and waterway. On the south shore near the ferry landing is Old House Creek. The deepest creek, Horsebend, originates toward the north end of the marsh and winds through the low marsh to terminate at open water near the waterway. Watermelon Creek originates near Horsebend and meanders west. Velvet Creek begins at Capers Inlet and flows with the tide to Lake Timicau.

Before Hurricane Hugo there was another creek, Horse Shoe Creek on earlier maps, wide and deep enough to allow passage of large yachts to a dock near the present Landings Building. Nearly obliterated by the storm, this creek now shows signs that it is restoring itself. At high tide it is clearly visible from the Landings Building.

The largest body of water in the interior of Dewees Island is Old House Lagoon, the impoundment. When a dike was built along Dewees Inlet Drive, spillways were provided over Old House Creek, and in 1993 they were replaced with a traditional rice trunk, permitting regulation of water level in the impoundment.

The most fully and frequently described part of the Dewees landscape is its beach. From the island's earliest development, beach lots were sold first and at substantially higher prices than interior "ocean view" property. Nearly every visitor is first taken to the beach, and renters may rate their trip in terms of how much time they have spent on the beach.

How do we account for the central place the beach has in our minds? Some have said that the ocean awakens an ancestral memory. Whether the ocean beach is stored in our subconscious, the beach experience is treasured. One major reason is surely observing and hearing the action of the waves. Whether they barely touch the shore on a windless day or roll in with foamy crests or crash ashore during a storm, the waves are always changing, always exciting. Oceanfront colors provide visual attraction. The blue of the sky, the varied blue and gray-green of the water and the whiteness of the sand charm our sight. And for sun lovers, few experiences can be more pleasant than lying on a beach blanket or in a reclining chair and allowing the sun's rays, regardless of the risk of skin cancer, to provide a natural tan.

Planting on beach. *Courtesy of Karl Ohlandt.*

These are attractions of all ocean beaches. The Dewees beach provides something more. One of these is spaciousness. Dewees Island's beach is more than two miles long, and at the north and south extremities it is over a quarter-mile wide. Even on the most popular days of summer, there is never an experience of crowding.

The Dewees beach is white sand and nearly level at the ocean's edge. This is attractive for walking or jogging and for shell seeking. There is not any armoring on the beach, but recent storms have left tree branches and trunks along the shore. The beach sand is not raked, and removing occasional litter is left to the user. Detritus from the marsh (spartina grass) swept out by ebb tide forms wrack lines at high tides. Above the wrack lines the dunes begin and continue into the bordering woodland and shrubbery.

Each year the residents of one or more South Carolina barrier islands have been sufficiently alarmed by beach erosion to prompt newspaper coverage. In the spring of 2007 it was Isle of Palms. Thanks to their setback from the ocean, Dewees Island homes have not been threatened. Walkers on the Dewees beach, though, have observed dunes that have been broken or washed away, sand fences wrecked and boardwalks abruptly ending at the top of dunes, leaving a steep drop to the water's edge. The walker also has seen beaches widen as sand is added.

Statistics may be found indicating that Dewees Island has a history of beach erosion. Reports have been published that between 1941 and 1973 the central and southern shore eroded nine hundred feet. The best response to these gloomy announcements is a walk to the seashore from the oceanfront houses. Severe as the recent erosion has been, it does not begin to damage the island's extensive dune system.

It is apparent that Dewees Island is vulnerable to erosion due to its small size, shoal location and the presence of forceful inlets. Explanations may be provided for the causes of erosion and accretion, but they do not provide a guide to forecasting future changes in the Dewees beach. Erosion statistics of the past are not a basis for predicting the future.

A geomorphology study has been commissioned by the Deedee Paschal Barrier Island Trust. This study records the beach and dune position every other month, with the purpose of learning with greater assurance the causes of beach erosion and accretion. Neither this study nor any other can be expected to predict the future beach changes. Dewees Island property owners are continuing the programs of beach and dune conservation that were undertaken after the disaster of Hurricane Hugo. Detritus is left where the tides deposit it, encouraging the collection of sand and thereby starting new dunes. Planting of beach vegetation including sea oats and beach amaranth helps to stabilize the beach. Sand fences are placed in critical locations, and all access to the beach is by boardwalks built over dunes. These measures cannot assure beach and dune stability, but in concert with natural beach processes, they help promote beach sustainability.

Chapter 3

Dewees Island's Natural History

The Soill near the Sea is more sandie than elsewhere, the foundation generally clay or clay and sand mixed together, but the best way to discover the soill is by its product. When wee came here wee found growing most of the timber that is in Ingland, as Oak of all sorts, Ash, Beech, etc., besid Cedar, Higuery, Chincopie and several other trees which afford our hogs abundance of fruit when their berries fall.

In all parts of the rivers and creeks, wee never want fish of severall sorts, which wee and our Indians doe catch with netts, hooks, weirs and by shooting them with arrowes. The fish wee have are Sturgeon, Bass, Drum, Mullet, Plaice, Trouts, Jacks, Catfish. Venison is no rarity to us unless about the Towne. Those who live toward the Indian parts of the settlements have brought them by one Indian in one year 100 sometimes 200 deer. Turkes also, and in the winter wild goose and dukes are to be found in great numbers.
—Maurice Mathews, A Contemporary View of Carolina in 1680, reproduced as written

More than three centuries have passed since Mathews first saw and described coastal Carolina. Many changes in plant and animal life have occurred, both on the sea islands and throughout the state. Most histories pass over these changes without comment. They are not as dramatic as battles or population movements. This history of Dewees Island is an attempt to look at what has happened on the island since it was first settled, and this includes change or continuity in the animal and plant life.

It would be impractical and tedious to mention each individual variety. At the same time it would not be satisfactory to provide only a general statement. The following discussion treats a limited number of varieties, focusing on those that are especially widespread and prominent or of particular importance to investigators.

Grasses, Shrubs and Trees

Writing in 1802, South Carolina's governor, John Drayton, listed the principal plants and trees of the coastal islands: "small pines and bay trees, live oaks, cedar, palmetto cabbage, silk grass, myrtle, cassena, wild olive, tooth-ache tree, prickly pear, seaside oats, and scattering coarse saline grasses." These grew on the islands before the first settlers arrived and are still among the most plentiful of island trees and plants.

It is impossible to imagine Dewees Island marshes without the spartina (smooth cord grass). This marsh grass provides nutrients for the insects and marine life that originate and mature in the marsh. It furnishes nesting and breeding places for wild fowl. It filters pollutants and holds the sediment that flows through the marsh waterways. It reduces the destructive force of storm-driven floodwater. Quite simply, the marsh cannot exist without the spartina grass, and could not otherwise have come into being. The early naturalists referred casually to spartina, describing it simply as a coarse marsh grass, perhaps with little awareness of its crucial place in the life of the marsh. Thousands of acres of marsh were subsequently filled or drained until public awareness of the grasses led to legislation protecting the marsh. On Dewees Island, the spartina remains, as it has from the earlier days, the most prominent and important of the marsh grasses.

The sea oat has nearly as vital a role in forming and preserving island dunes as spartina has in building and protecting the marsh. Sea oats are mentioned by pioneering naturalists as part of island flora, but without much awareness of their ecological importance. For years, sea oats were cut and collected by residents and tourists for dried arrangements. In his description of Edisto Island in 1827, the botanist Lewis Gibbes wrote that cattle were uprooting sea oats from the island dunes. Ultimately, it was recognized that sea oats were among the principal protectors of the dunes. Resistant to salt, sea oats grow on dunes closest to high tide and help maintain the dunes from erosion. South Carolina law now prohibits the removal of sea oats from public land, and Dewees Island also protects the plant. Property owners and Dewees staff have planted thousands of sea oats throughout the dunes. It can be fairly assumed that sea oats are as widespread on Dewees today as when the island was first settled.

Among the most common and widely found shrubs on South Carolina barrier islands is the wax myrtle. It is relatively salt-tolerant, enabling it to grow at the edges of dunes and marsh, as well as in the maritime forest. On Dewees Island, wax myrtle often grows in near impenetrable thickets.

The wax myrtle was known to the coastal American Indians and European settlers, and was thought to have varied uses. One early and continuing use is in wax candles. Bayberry candles were regarded as superior to those made of tallow and were probably the most familiar type of candle in colonial America. Myrtle leaves were also used to produce a tea, and the bark found medical applications in relieving diarrhea and as a cold remedy. The names given to the shrub by observers throughout the years—sweet myrtle, sweet bay, bayberry, waxberry, wild tea, tea box, meckle, mucklebush and candleberry tree—indicate the common beliefs in its uses and properties. On Dewees Island, the wax myrtle can be found in all areas. Small birds favor its nutlets and are frequently seen flitting from branch to branch.

Yaupon holly grows on Dewees at the edges of the marsh, and throughout the maritime forest. Yaupon was known to the earliest European settlers and its medicinal properties were highly praised. Thomas Ashe wrote early in the eighteenth century:

> There grows in Carolina the famous Cassiny, whose admirable and incomparable Virtues are highly applauded and extolled by French and Spanish Writers. It is the Leaves of a certain Tree, which boyl'd [sic] in Water (as we do Thea [sic]) wonderfully enliven and invigorate the Heart with genuine easy Sweats and Transpirations preserving the Mind free and serene keeping the Body fresh, active and lively, not for an hour, or two but for as many days as those Authors report, without any Nourishment or Subsistence, which, if true, is really admirable.

Naturalists John Lawson and Marc Catesby described the cultivation and use of yaupon by coastal American Indians. (Lawson observed that the holly name was yaupon in North Carolina and cassina in South Carolina, but yaupon now seems to be the generally accepted name.) Yaupon leaves and twigs were dried and crushed, and after adding water, they made a black beverage that was consumed in large quantities at tribal gatherings. It is not hallucinatory, but it contains a considerable amount of caffeine and if drunk in excess, induces vomiting. Despite this emetic property, yaupon was sought by American Indians throughout the southeast. The coastal American Indians traded its leaves to other tribes, and yaupon holly plants now grow in the Piedmont and as far west as the Great Smoky Mountains.

Coastal American Indians used many other native plants and trees as food or seasoning, and the early European settlers quickly learned what to enjoy and what to avoid. Dewees Island today has edible plants numerous enough to fill a cookbook with recipes using Dewees delicacies. Yaupon holly is not an ingredient, but among the native plants used in Dewees Island cooking are samphire, dollar weed, yucca, sea rocket, cattail hearts, prickly pear and mallow.

Three hundred years ago, African slaves brought to Carolina a knowledge of sweetgrass basket making. That knowledge has been passed on, but sweetgrass has become scarce. Sweetgrass grows on Dewees Island, and in 1992 the island entered a program with the Mount Pleasant Sweetgrass Basket Makers Association. Dewees permits basket makers to harvest grass on the island, and in exchange the basket makers teach the fundamentals to island residents at a special workshop, where they display their baskets.

Governor Drayton and early naturalists reported the widespread presence of live oak trees throughout the South Carolina coastal plain, and they were certainly common on Dewees Island before European settlement. Native Americans hunted deer and turkey under the forest canopy, and ate the same oak acorns that attracted the game. Live oak remains present on the coast and most barrier islands, including Dewees, and can grow to great size. Nature at its most violent may tear branches and strip away leaves, but usually the tree still stands. As the live oak grows, its trunk twists giving added strength and toughness. Tree branches stretch out from the main trunk providing support and forcing winds up and over the treetops and adjoining buildings. Live oak timbers were used for warship construction during the War of 1812, and after the war's end a "live oak mania" led to the felling of great stands of trees. The oldest live oaks on Dewees are almost certainly secondary growth.

Another Dewees Island tree that has shown itself resistant to hurricane winds is the cabbage palmetto. Its multitude of finger-like roots cling to the sand and its flexible trunk bends with the wind, rather than breaking. Its fronds do not form a canopy, which might intercept gales and topple the tree. Palmettos on Dewees line the ocean coast behind the dunes, and are scattered through the maritime forest and shrub thickets. They grew on the island before the arrival of the first Europeans, and while logged during the eighteenth and nineteenth centuries, they have never been considered to be threatened.

Dewees Island has a vegetation management plan regarding cutting or trimming trees. Dewees also has an affirmative plan for replenishing beach vegetation, planting trees in nature areas and planting and tending wildflowers.

The evidence supports a conclusion that the varieties of vegetation found on Dewees Island before its settlement around 1700 still thrive on the island. Some species of trees, most notably the Chinese tallow (or popcorn berry) tree, have been introduced in recent years. Efforts are being made to eradicate this invasive species. In most respects the trees and shrubs found on Dewees Island today are those that were found by the earliest inhabitants.

Birds

In the early years of the twentieth century, Arthur Wayne was among the most respected and best-known American ornithologists. Wayne lived on Porcher's Bluff, north of Mount Pleasant. He could look across the marsh to Dewees Island, and was a frequent visitor to Dewees. In addition to observation and description of coastal birds, Wayne wrote of changes in bird population over the centuries since humans first settled the South Carolina coast and sea islands. Here is an authority who can give a firsthand report on South Carolina's bird life a century ago, allowing comparison of past and present on Dewees.

When Wayne wrote, the passenger pigeon and Carolina parakeet, which had once been widespread in coastal South Carolina, were extinct. The ivory-billed woodpecker, described by Marc Catesby in the early eighteenth century as a coastal resident, had vanished from the Carolinas. Unregulated and widespread hunting was the cause of the extinction of these birds and the near loss of other varieties.

Wayne identified bird varieties that were endangered. For some of these birds the danger has passed or is greatly reduced. The great egret and snowy egret had been hunted since the nineteenth century for feathers used to decorate women's hats. It was the use of bird plumage and of the bodies of small birds on clothing that aroused public indignation and led directly to the founding of the National Audubon Society. The near extinction of egrets and other threatened bird varieties prompted legislation that banned the hunting of them. Both the great and snowy egrets inhabit Dewees Island, probably in increasing numbers.

Wayne mentioned the brown pelican as endangered, and reported theft of eggs as a likely cause of its depletion. Later research identified the use of DDT insecticide as the threat to the pelican, and to the osprey and bald eagle as well. The DDT resulted in thin, fragile eggshells and a low survival rate of young birds. Prohibition of the use of DDT and related pesticides saved these birds. Both the pelican and the osprey are commonly found on Dewees Island.

The Dewees Island bird checklist includes numerous tern varieties found on Dewees, among them the least tern. Like the egrets, the least tern was relentlessly hunted until the beginning of the twentieth century. Legal restrictions have provided some protection for these birds. The principal menace for terns today, and for Wilson's plover as well, is the loss of habitat resulting from development of beaches and the increasing human and animal traffic. Terns and plover nest in colonies on ocean beaches, and their nesting locations are lost as humans occupy a beach. On Dewees, tern nesting areas are roped off and beach walkers are warned by painted signs of the proximity of tern nests. (The terns repeat this warning by flying close overhead.) So far, this tern population does not appear diminished.

The loss of habitat is probably a greater threat to grassland species of birds than it is to water and shorebirds. The Audubon report in 2004 on the state of birds asserts that 85 percent of species of grassland birds are declining. The report sets out the reasons for the decline, essentially the same reasons that threaten the barrier island ecosystems. As trees are cut and undergrowth cleared for house building, as grass is planted for lawns and golf courses, as pesticides are applied and fallen leaves removed and as freshwater wetlands are drained, birds no longer find food and refuge. Although the Dewees land management policy protects the migratory birds, the numbers visiting Dewees are inevitably affected by loss of habitat elsewhere.

In some instances, loss of other habitat has brought greater numbers to Dewees. Examples of birds that are probably more frequently seen are the wood stork and the white ibis, which have suffered loss of territory in Florida while increasing numbers appear in Georgia and South Carolina.

Dewees Island has sought to increase bird population by posting warning signs near bird nesting sites, by providing houses for martins and wood ducks and platforms for osprey and by encouraging the growth of plants that will provide food for birds. This program may be succeeding. Recent bird counts identified more than two hundred varieties, placing Dewees in line with international destinations for bird counts

Animals

Before the arrival of European colonists, South Carolina was home to a number of predatory animals. John Lawson reported seeing panther (cougar), wolves and wildcats. Although Lawson was not specific as to the location at which he found these animals, it is probable that they were seen on the coast as well as inland. Marc Catesby, the naturalist who explored the Ashley and Stono Rivers, also mentioned panthers, wolves and wildcats, as well as bear.

A century later, the number of predatory animals was greatly reduced. The cougar and bobcat had nearly disappeared, while the red wolf, then still the most numerous predator, was also vanishing from the coast. The decrease in predators took place as the South Carolina coast was settled. As fields were cleared and planted, the natural territory of woods and wetlands disappeared, taking from predators their habitat and forcing them to retreat to remaining, but constantly decreasing, wilderness.

Another perhaps even greater threat to predators was the coming of livestock. Coastal and island settlers brought with them domestic animals. John Lawson, traveling by canoe north from Charleston in 1700, spent his first night on Bell's Island, where the only resident was a caretaker employed to look after cattle and hogs. A century later, when Dewees Island was advertised for sale, one of its attractions was "an excellent range for horses, cattle, sheep, hogs and goats." Predators were a threat to the stock, and landowners actively hunted animals that preyed on domestic stock.

Owners' inability or failure to control domestic animals resulted, in many cases, in these animals returning to the wild. Dewees Island was largely uninhabited during the Civil War, and it is probable that the livestock were abandoned. By the time the Huylers bought the island in 1925, herds of feral cattle, goats and hogs roamed at large. Boar hunts rid the island of wild hogs, while the cattle and goats gradually disappeared. There no longer exist any feral domestic animals on Dewees Island.

There are indications that occasional predators are returning to Dewees. There have been a few sightings of bobcats, and on at least one occasion, observers are certain they saw a cougar. Tracks also indicate the presence of big cats. Newspaper reports confirm that cougars are found throughout the low country. For the foreseeable future, however, these predators will be scarce on the island.

There is another predator on Dewees Island, more numerous by far than all others combined. Alligators may be found in nearly every pond on Dewees, and their tracks seen in the sand of most roads. Their presence was noted by Huyler family members and by naturalist observers. We can be confident that alligators lived on Dewees Island long before the earliest humans arrived and will probably still be there as long as the island exists. If their territory is respected, there is little cause for concern.

Both John Lawson and Marc Catesby observed bison in low country South Carolina early in the eighteenth century, and Lawson saw elk, but probably in the more central part of the state or in North Carolina. These large animals vanished from the Carolinas before 1800 with the loss of wilderness.

Writing in 1680, Maurice Mathews observed that the deer population of coastal South Carolina was plentiful and provided venison to the settlers. In the half century that followed, the slaughter of deer reached extraordinary numbers. Deer were still killed for meat, but the greater number for skins that were shipped to England. Between 1717 and 1719, some 17–19,000 deerskins annually left Charles Town. By the mid-1720s the yearly total was 60,000, rising to 80,000 by the 1730s and 150,000 by mid-century. After 1750, the trade in deerskins dropped off. One reason was the increasing friction between Britain and its American colonies, with embargoes and interruptions of commerce between America and the mother country. Of greater significance was the decrease

Wild boar, 1970s. *Courtesy of Henry and Kitty Beard.*

in deer population due to overhunting and the loss of habitat. As land was cleared for the planting of crops, and the great pines were cut for the shipbuilding industry, the sheltering forests were lost and deer retreated to the Appalachian Mountains.

Unlike the elk and other large animals, the deer population of South Carolina did not vanish. Ultimately, the pendulum began its swing in the opposite direction. The boll weevil and a long drought caused the abandonment of millions of acres of cotton fields. Farmers moved to cities in South Carolina and elsewhere, and the land returned first to a wilderness, and later to suburban lawns and shrubbery, more favorable environments for deer. The U.S. Forest Service described the change: "By the 1960s and 1970s the pattern of forest, field and pasture was similar to that prior to 1800." Hunting is regulated by law and is prohibited in residential areas. In consequence, the population of white-tailed deer in South Carolina increased from several thousand in 1900 to 30–40,000 in the 1960s, and then to a million or more by the year 2000.

It seems reasonable to expect that the trend in South Carolina as a whole has been repeated on Dewees Island. Researchers have concluded that deer were present on Dewees during presettlement times. The Native Americans of the coast certainly hunted the white-tailed deer on Dewees before the first Europeans arrived. Probably the deer population suffered as farming became the economic life of the island. During and after the Civil War, the pastures and cultivated farms were abandoned, and Dewees began to return to wilderness. Deer were plentiful when the Huylers purchased Dewees and are frequently seen now.

A strategy for deer management is an integral part of the current development. Since the island philosophy is to avoid disturbing the natural environment, minimal interference with deer is assumed. On the other hand, unlimited increase in deer population affects other island values. The lack of predators and the temperate climate of Dewees could result in an exponential growth of the deer population. When deer numbers explode, native vegetation is destroyed and other animal species are denied habitat. In an effort to preserve a balance, limited hunting by professionals is allowed. Many residents deplore any deer hunting, but it seems unavoidable if the balance of nature is to be preserved.

Among the smaller animals, rabbits, squirrels, opossum and raccoon have been identified as being present on Dewees before European settlement. In later years they were joined by otters and by mink. Squirrels and opossum are no longer found on Dewees. During the time that the Huylers lived on this island rabbits were not present, but they have returned. The small animals of Dewees Island today are, in general, the same animals that Lawson reported seeing in South Carolina during his explorations. Lawson was particularly interested in the behavior of the raccoon, which he observed catching crabs with its tail and pulling fiddler crabs from their holes. He added that the raccoon is "the drunkest creature living, if he can get any liquor that is strong and sweet."

The absence of beaver on Dewees may result from the lack of freshwater streams, while the disappearance of opossum and squirrel seems likely to have been caused by hurricanes and tidal surges that inundated the island. An unexplained phenomenon is the return of rabbits after their absence during the Huyler residence.

Dewees Island does not have a program for controlling small animal populations. Some small animals, especially raccoons, are present in unpleasantly large numbers. Their native fear of humans is outweighed by the comfort of water, food and shelter found in homes.

State naturalists have reintroduced a small animal, the mink, which formerly was plentiful along the South Carolina coast. Several marsh mink have been released on Dewees and are reported to be breeding. Questions may be raised about the wisdom of human intervention in environmental processes. The mink is described as a vicious little animal with a taste for marsh hens and their eggs. On the other hand, the mink also eats marsh rats. Apparently, only experience will show whether the arrival of mink will be positive or negative to the island.

Every year female loggerhead turtles return to the barrier islands, including Dewees, to leave eggs. The nests of turtles are threatened by predators, chiefly raccoons and ghost crabs, by high tides flooding the nests and by human intrusion. Since 1999 Dewees has been a site-certified turtle island, responsible for identifying and protecting turtle nests. Dewees Island residents and their guests have participated actively in this program, walking the beach in the spring and summer months to locate nests, checking

Turtle tracks. *Courtesy of Jill Cochrane.*

thereafter to be sure the nests are not disturbed and the warning signs are in place and assisting newly hatched turtles to reach the surf.

Preservation of plant and animal life on Dewees Island has been an essential part of Dewees development. Neither hunting (except for the Deer Management Program) nor other killing of wildlife is permitted. Except for nonnative varieties such as the Chinese tallow, trees and plants may not be removed without Architectural Resource Board approval. A large part of the island is permanently set aside as a wildlife preserve. Native shrubs and flowers are planted. As a result of policies such as these, the development of Dewees Island has benefited the native plant and animal life.

1. Aerial view of Dewees Island. *Courtesy of Jonathan Lutz.*

2. Dewees Island oceanfront houses. *Courtesy of Jonathan Lutz.*

3. Dewees Island marsh houses. *Courtesy of Jill Cochrane.*

4. Beach embankment broken by Hurricane David, 1979. *Courtesy of Bobby Kennedy.*

5. Dewees ferry, *Aggie Gray. Courtesy of Brucie Harry.*

6. The Huyler House. *Courtesy of Karl Ohlandt.*

7. Dewees Island Landings Building. *Courtesy of Jill Cochrane.*

8. Barge delivering building materials. *Courtesy of Judy Fairchild.*

9. Island road. *Courtesy of Kathy Warren.*

10. Submarine tower. *Courtesy of Joseph McAlhany Jr.*

11. Dunes with sea oats. *Courtesy of Judy Fairchild.*

12. Fisherman. *Courtesy of Wharton Winstead.*

13. "Crab Dock" ©2003. *Painting by Diane K. Kliros. Courtesy of Bill and Tish Easterlin.*

14. Boardwalk
leading to beach.
*Courtesy of Judy
Fairchld.*

15. "Bubba's View: February 2000" ©2000. *Painting by Kathryn Banks.*

16. Young, enthusiastic crabbers. *Courtesy of Judy Fairchild.*

17. Camp kids studying marsh. *Courtesy of Judy Fairchild.*

18. Parade on July Fourth. *Courtesy of Peter Cotton.*

19. Duck hunters (before 1990). *Courtesy of Edmund Frampton.*

20. Visiting grandchildren on July Fourth. *Courtesy of Peter Cotton.*

21. Raccoon. *Courtesy of Joseph McAlhany Jr.*

Above: 22. "Family Gathering"
©2006. *Courtesy of Wharton Winstead.*

Left: 23. Osprey family. *Courtesy of Jill Cochrane.*

Top: 24. Birds gathering on beach. *Courtesy of Wharton Winstead.*

Middle: 25. Wood storks in impoundment. *Courtesy of Esther Doyle.*

Right: 26. Roseate spoonbill. *Courtesy of Janet Kennedy.*

Left: 27. Heron on dead tree. *Courtesy of Wharton Winstead.*

Middle: 28. Baby turtles reach the surf. *Courtesy of Gary McGraw.*

Bottom: 29. Lake Timicau. *Photo by John McLeod.*

30. "On Chapel Pond" ©2003. *Painting by Diane K. Kilros. Courtesy of Allen and Cozy Mitchell.*

31. "Dewees Island Creek" ©2001. *Painting by Kathryn Banks.*

32. Sunrise on Dewees. *Courtesy of Joseph McAlhany Jr.*

33. Yaupon holly. *Courtesy of Karl Ohlandt.*

34. Evening primrose. *Courtesy of Karl Ohlandt.*

35. Glasswort. *Courtesy of Karl Ohlandt.*

Top: 36. Marsh mallow. *Courtesy of Karl Ohlandt.*

Middle: 37. Sweetgrass. *Courtesy of Karl Ohlandt.*

Bottom: 38. *Painting by Margaret Hilton. Courtesy of Patty Alexander.*

Chapter 4

Barrier Island Discovery and Settlement

They are really better to us, than we are to them; they always give us Victuals at their Quarters, and take care we are arm'd against Hunger and Thirst. We do not so by them (generally speaking) but let them walk by our Doors Hungry, and do not often relieve them. We look upon them with Scorn and Disdain, and think them little better than Beasts in Human Shape, though if well examined, we shall find that, for all our Religion and Education, we possess more Moral Deformities, and Evils than these Savages do, or are acquainted withal.

—*John Lawson,* A New Voyage to Carolina, *1709*

While there is a good deal of evidence that Native Americans lived in what is now South Carolina as long ago as ten thousand years, it is unlikely that they settled along the coast. Beginning about three thousand years ago, however, others did move to the ocean shore. Earliest to arrive were those now referred to as Woodlands people. They settled principally along the coast between Cape Fear and the Savannah River. At one time they may have spoken a single language, but when European explorers first met them, at least two languages and a number of dialects were spoken. By the time of European arrival, the Woodlands people had separated into tribes. Estimates differ as to the number of tribes or nations formed, but it was at least twelve and perhaps as many as twenty. Many geographic locations along the South Carolina coast—among them Wando, Stono, Edisto, Bohicket, Kiawah, Ashepoo and Combahee—are names of Woodlands nations.

Estimates of the number of American Indians living along the coast before the arrival of Europeans vary substantially. Gene Waddell, writing in *Indians of the South Carolina Lowcountry*, estimated that the Native American population of the coast from the Santee to the Savannah River was at most only 1,750. His figure was based on a census of individual tribes, and it omitted the tribes not included in the census. Timothy Silver, in *A New Face on the Countryside*, concluded that in 1685, more than a century after the earliest European settlements, the American Indian population along the South

Carolina coast was ten thousand, but decreased rapidly after that time. Regardless of the exact number, it seems clear that Woodlands people had ample space to live, hunt and raise crops.

There were four sources of food, some more abundant than others. Some sources were available year-round, while others were seasonal. The availability of these foods helped determine the domestic life of the coastal nations. During the summer months, people lived in small communities and relied principally on crops they raised. Corn, usually two plantings a year, pumpkins and melons were principal agricultural products. Fish and shellfish were plentiful all along the coast and were a second major food source. A third source was venison and other game. After the growing season many coastal Native Americans left their communities and migrated inland. There they survived by hunting and by gathering nuts and roots, a fourth source of food. Village life ceased and families moved separately through the forest.

In large measure the coastal American Indians lived in peace with their neighboring tribes, carried on trade and reported their news at intertribal gatherings. They did not form permanent alliances with other nations. Threats from external enemies could produce joint action, but when a crisis passed, nations returned to their separate lives. Before the arrival of Europeans, the principal enemies of the coastal Native Americans were people of the river valleys. The most hostile were the Westo living along the Savannah River.

Only a few years after the voyages of Columbus to the Caribbean, Spanish explorers and aspiring colonizers were again on their way to the New World, this time to the North American mainland. After a landing in Florida, Spanish ships proceeded north, bringing the first Europeans to see the marshes and barrier islands of Carolina. In 1514 a West Indian planter, Lucas Vásquez de Ayllón, dispatched a ship that cruised as far north as Cape Fear and made a brief landing at some point along the coast. In 1521, he directed another expedition remembered principally for enslaving American Indians, who rashly accepted an invitation to tour the ship. This landing was at Waccamaw Neck near the present Georgetown, and the captured American Indians were either Sewees or their near neighbors, the Waccamaws. A third Carolina trip was to Santa Elena where a settlement was founded that remained on and off in existence for the next fifty years. A year after the Santa Elena settlement, a landing at Winyah Bay was followed by establishing a town at Waccamaw. However, within six months this settlement was abandoned. Cold weather, fever, starvation and Native American hostility contributed to the failure of the Waccamaw venture. Thereafter, Spanish settlement in South Carolina was limited to the Santa Elena town and fort, except for a brief landing in 1561 at present-day McClellanville. It seems that Spanish efforts to colonize the northern part of South Carolina were brief and remembered afterward chiefly for the Native Americans' anger against the invader.

The sixteenth century was marked by competing efforts of France and Spain to occupy parts of North America. Along the southern Atlantic coast the Spanish presence dominated. French explorers and colonizers settled north and west, and they undertook only one substantial venture on the Carolina coast. This was a settlement named Charlesfort, at Port Royal. Lacking sufficient food, this colony was abandoned in 1562. From time to time in later years, when the English claimed and settled Carolina, France launched unsuccessful military threats, but these never suggested an interest in colonization or political conquest.

England had not participated in the sixteenth-century struggle between Spain and France for dominance in America. It was only after successfully resisting Spanish invasion and taking an increasing military and political role on the European continent that England undertook settlement in the New World. This venture began in areas such as Virginia, which had not previously been settled by Spain or France, but before many years had passed the English colonial effort extended to contested territory.

England's political claim to land south of Virginia was based on its sponsorship in 1497 of a voyage of discovery by John Cabot. Records are sparse as to Cabot's southern journey, but England claimed that it had included Carolina. In the early years of the seventeenth century, England asserted its claim to Carolina, and at the conclusion of the English civil wars, Charles II named proprietors of the colony and encouraged discovery and settlement.

The earliest of English explorations was led by William Hilton, a resident of Barbados. He sailed as far north as Cape Fear, then turned south, landing in St. Helena's Sound, near Port Royal, an area then populated by Edisto Indians and a few Spanish settlers at Santa Elena. Hilton's discussions with the Native Americans were conducted in an atmosphere of mutual suspicion. Hilton did not make any effort to go ashore north of Port Royal, but he did sail again to Cape Fear, then returned to Barbados and reported his trip in glowing terms.

Influenced by Hilton's report, several English groups established a colony near Cape Fear. Under direction of the proprietors, plans were then made for establishing another settlement somewhere south of Cape Romain. Matters progressed to the point that an exploratory fleet departed from Barbados in 1665. Storms at Cape Fear and the destruction of a ship led to abandonment of this project. Interest however remained high for increasing settlement in Carolina and establishing once and for all English dominance of the Atlantic coast north of Florida.

In 1666, Robert Sandford, a planter living in the Cape Fear area, began a voyage to carry out the proprietors' desire for a settlement south of Cape Romain. After a brief landing at the site of the present town of Rockville, South Carolina, he sailed to Port Royal where Hilton had landed three years earlier. Sandford received a warm welcome from the American Indian inhabitants, more cordial than Hilton had been accorded. He was favorably impressed by the rich land of St. Helena's Island and by the good harbor there. After a visit of several days, the Sandford party continued their expedition by sailing up the South Edisto River. Again Sandford was welcomed, this time by the Edisto Indians, who urged him to enter the Kiawah River, the river now known as the Ashley. Sandford indicated an interest in the area, but missed the river entrance as he sailed north along the coast, and by the time the error was discovered it was too late to return. At the conclusion of his journey, Sandford strongly recommended Port Royal as the site of an English settlement.

In 1669, Lord Ashley Cooper, one of the original proprietors, raised money in England to purchase three ships that would travel with settlers to Carolina. Storms destroyed one ship and blew another off course. One vessel, the *Carolina*, reached the South Carolina coast, landing at Sewee Bay adjoining Bull Island. Here the ship's crew and prospective settlers had their first meeting with Sewee Indians. A passenger, Nicholas Carteret, described the greeting:

> *Upon* [the ship's] *approach to ye Land few were ye nations who upon ye Strand made fires & came towards us ye whooping in their own tone & manner making signs also where we should Land, & when we came ashore they stroaked us on ye shoulders with their hands saying Bony Conraro Angles, knowing us to be English by our colleurs (as wee supported) we then gave them Brass rings & tobacco at which they seemed well pleased....as we to ye shore a good number of Indians appeared clad with deare skins having with them their bows & arrows, but one Indian calling out Appado they withdrew & lodged their bows & returning ran up to ye middle in mire and watter to carry us a shoare where when we came they gave us ye stroaking Complint, of ye country.*

Following this landing, the English and their Sewee hosts journeyed to a nearby Native American village. Leaders of the colonizing group made it known to the Sewee that their destination was Port Royal, the location recommended by Sandford. In response, the Sewee reported that Port Royal had been raided by the hostile Westo Indians and the settlement destroyed. They went on to say that the Kiawah River site previously proposed to Sandford was a more secure location and offered as good conditions for settlement as any. The travelers were interested but apparently not fully persuaded, for the *Carolina* sailed from Sewee Bay to Port Royal, then to St. Helena and only last to the Ashley River. There they founded the community of Charles Town.

Contemporary descriptions of the Sewee have been left by Carteret and by the surveyor naturalist John Lawson, who traveled by canoe and on foot through the Sewee territory in 1701. Sewee occupied the largest area of any coastal Native American tribe, extending from the Santee River south to the Wando. Both Carteret and Lawson commented on the courtesy and kindness of the Sewee. Little gestures, such as carrying the English visitors across muddy waters and use of the word *appado* (peace) were signs of the friendly character of those American Indians. But courtesy alone was not the reason for the Sewee encouraging the English to found a settlement close to their territory. The prospect of trade was certainly influential. Sewee had previously carried on commerce with inland tribes. Smoked fish had been exchanged for brass and other metal objects. A lively trade would develop with the residents of Charles Town. Thousands of deer and other animal skins were delivered in exchange for manufactured articles brought from England. Native Americans were keenly aware of the number of English ships entering and leaving the harbor and the volume of goods carried back and forth between Carolina and the mother country.

Another reason the Sewee urged the first English to settle near their territory was the security they hoped would come from the colony. Sewee were familiar with the Spanish occupation, its deceit and brutality and the taking of slaves. Spanish ships had cruised the Carolina coast, while shore parties passed through the Sewee territory. Of still greater concern was the Westo tribe of the Savannah River. Westo were reputed to be cannibals, and they were certainly savage warriors. A fortification and town along the river to the south held by friendly neighbors would be a strong defense.

The English as well as their Native American allies were concerned by the possibilities of attack, either by hostile tribes or by the Spanish or French. Anxiety regarding hostile ships led to establishment of watchtowers on the barrier islands. As early as 1674 a tower was authorized on Sullivan's Island. Captain Florence O'Sullivan was named lookout and instructed to fire a cannon on the approach of any ship. O'Sullivan has been described as a rude and unpleasant person, and living alone on the island named for him was probably to his liking. In later years, lookouts were posted at the north and south ends of Long Island and the south tip of Bull Island. Two Englishmen and two American Indians with a canoe manned each lookout. There is not any report of a lookout tower on Dewees or Capers Islands.

The settlers' concerns were not imaginary. Spanish and French conducted a joint raid in 1680, but failed in their invasion. Rather than attack Charles Town, a force landed at Mount Pleasant across the marsh from Long and Dewees Islands. Settlers and their Sewee allies captured some of the landing party, while others retreated to their ships and sailed away. In 1686 a Spanish force landed on Edisto Island with the intent of capturing Charles Town, but a major hurricane frustrated its efforts. In 1706, two French ships landed at Sewee Bay and troops crossed Mount Pleasant to Remley's Point. Charles Town militia attacked the invaders and pursued them to Porcher's Bluff, where a part of the invading force was captured or killed.

Unlike other coastal American Indian tribes, the Sewee were not known to have moved inland during the winter months. While agriculture may have been difficult in the winter, fish and game were available at all seasons, and the Sewee were noted hunters and fishermen. Deer were probably the preferred game. Hunters could disguise themselves as deer and deceive the animals and even other hunters. Other wildlife hunted by the Sewee were bear, wild boar, raccoon and beaver. Apart from providing food and clothing for the Sewee, sale and trade of skins with the colonists was an important part of the Native American economy. Little is known about the social life of the Sewee people, but it has been remarked that they had a democratic government in which women participated and shared ownership of land and chattels.

Although the name "Sewee" is translated as "island people," it is probable that the Sewee never lived on Dewees or the other islands between the Cooper and Santee Rivers. There is no record of any American Indian nation living on a South Carolina barrier island until 1685, when the Edisto Indians moved from their village on the Ashley River to Edisto Island. Island soil was not satisfactory for growing corn, and the dense undergrowth on the islands was an obstacle to any agriculture. Further, storms could arrive with little warning, and the islands did not provide any refuge from storm surge. Although the Sewee did not have any island village, they did visit Dewees and the other islands between the Cooper and Santee Rivers on a regular basis. There was good reason for the Native American people to call them the "Hunting Islands." Mounds of shells found on Dewees show that the islands were rich in shellfish and that festivals were probably held after hunting or fishing expeditions. The present village of Awendaw takes its name from a Sewee settlement, perhaps the one visited by the voyagers on the *Carolina*. Enormous mounds of shells and abundant pottery shards on Porcher's Bluff indicate that a village may have existed there. The last known habitation of the Sewee was on the Santee River, and no remnant of it exists. It is remembered only as the place of the last census count of the Sewee people.

The Sewee nation existed for fewer than fifty years after the English arrival. Disease, especially smallpox transmitted first by the Spanish and later by the English, wiped out entire villages. John Lawson wrote:

> *These Sewee had been formerly a large Nation, though now very much decreased, since the English hath settled their Land, and all other nations of Indians are observed to partake of the same Fate where the Europeans came, the Indians being a People very apt to catch any Distemper, they are afflicted withal.*

It has been reported that toward the end of the seventeenth century, another disaster befell the remains of the Sewee nation. It had long been observed by the Sewee that goods unloaded in Charles Town from English ships were sold to the Native Americans, and that deerskins were then loaded into the same ships for shipment from Charles Town. It occurred to the Sewee that more favorable terms might be obtained if the Native Americans dealt directly with the English. To accomplish this objective, large canoes were built and boarded by the best oarsmen of the nation. Those canoes were paddled into the Atlantic Ocean, where they disappeared. It was later learned that the canoes were destroyed in a storm, and that the survivors were taken by an English ship and sold as slaves in the West Indies. This report was first made by John Lawson, who traveled through the Sewee country a few years later. It has been repeated by historians and other writers and seems authentic.

The number of Sewee was never large, probably not exceeding one thousand. As a result of disease, warfare and the canoe tragedy, only fifty-four were counted in a census of 1712. After the Yemassee War of 1715–16, the Sewee nation vanished, along with the other coastal American Indian tribes. Possibly they traveled to the territory of the Catawba Indians in North Carolina, but if so they soon lost their identity. The coastal Native Americans are remembered only in geographic place names. As a final irony, the five Hunting Islands have lost their Sewee names. No one knows what Sullivan's Island and Isle of Palms were named, while the islands once called Timicau, Hawan and Oni See Cau are now Dewees, Capers and Bull. It is a sad end for a gracious and valiant people.

Chapter 5

The Island Called Timicau

On December the 28th, 1700, I began my voyage [for North Carolina] from Charles-Town, being six Englishmen in company, with three Indian-men, and one Woman, Wife of our Indian-Guide…. At 4 in the Afternoon (at half Flood) we pass'd with our Canoe over the Breach, leaving Sullivan's Island on our Starboard…. At Night we got to Bell's Island, a poor Spot of Land, being about ten Miles round, where liv'd (at that Time) a Bermudian, being employ'd here with a Boy, to look after a Stock of Cattle and Hogs, by the Owner of this Island. One Side of the Roof of his House was thatched with Palmeto-leaves, the other open to the Heavens, thousands of Musketoes and other troublesome Insects, tormenting both Man and Beast inhabiting these Islands…. We took up our Lodging that Night with the Bermudian; our Entertainment was very indifferent, there being no fresh Water to be had on the Island.
—John Lawson, Journal, 1709, reproduced as written

Early Colonial History

John Lawson was clearly unhappy with the night he spent on Bell's Island, wherever it might have been. This name does not appear on any other record, and opinions differ regarding its identity. Some historians have concluded that Bell's Island is Isle of Palms, the island directly north of Sullivan's Island, while others favor Dewees Island. Lawson's comment that the island was "about ten Miles round" seems to describe more correctly the circumference of Dewees.

In 1700 the owner of Dewees, and of Capers and Bull Islands, was a Charles Town resident, Thomas Cary. He was a prosperous merchant, and owner of several ships. Politically he was active, having been appointed secretary of the province, a member of the grand council and receiver general. He was also register of the first vice admiralty court and a colonel of the militia. Perhaps more significantly, Cary was the son-in-law of John Archdale, and Archdale was a very important person. Indeed, John Archdale may have been the *most* important person in Charles Town as governor of Carolina and a lord proprietor of the colony. As a proprietor, Archdale was in position to obtain from the king grants for land in Carolina.

When England claimed ownership of colonies in America, the king had to decide whether to govern directly or appoint proprietors as his representatives. King Charles I, who claimed Carolina for England, had little knowledge of the land or how it might be developed. The proprietor he appointed to manage colonization, Sir Robert Heath, had little more understanding. Only when Charles II became ruler and named new proprietors more familiar with colonial management did successful settlement occur.

Sir William Berkeley, one of Charles's proprietors, died in 1669, leaving the proprietary interest to his widow. She sold her interest to John Archdale, a wealthy and prominent English Quaker. In 1695 Archdale was named governor of Carolina and moved to Charles Town.

Shortly after Archdale's arrival, Cary turned to his father-in-law for assistance in the purchase of land. Archdale did not disappoint him. During the proprietary period land in Carolina could be purchased through the assistance of a proprietor, by a royal grant. A surveyor would plat a tract of land and have the plat certified by a deputy surveyor or by the surveyor general of the colony. The certified grant then constituted a royal grant. In 1696 Archdale arranged a survey of Sessions (as Capers was then known) and Jimicau (a variation of Timicau). A year later royal grants were issued to Thomas Cary for these islands. At more or less the same time, Cary purchased 1,580 acres on Bull Island from Samuel Hartley. Cary thus became owner of the northern three Hunting Islands.

Cary never personally occupied the islands he had acquired, employing the "Bermudian" on Timicau and an "honest Scot" on Sessions to manage livestock and defend against trespassers. He sold Sessions Island in 1702 to William Capers and Bull Island in 1706 to John Collins. At about the same time he sold Timicau to Roger Player, and it subsequently passed to a succession of owners:

1710—From Player to John Butler and John Givens.
1711—Butler's ownership share to Givens.
1714—From Givens to Charles Hill.
Ownership gap.
1750—From William Hendricks to James Withers.
1756—From James Withers to Richard Withers, and from Withers to Arnoldus Vanderhorst.

Then, following another gap, the island known as Timicau was conveyed to Cornelius Dewees, perhaps as early as 1761.

The Dewees Family in America

Most of the known history of the Dewees family has been collected by the Dewees Family Association and reported in Dewees/Deweese newsletters. Information about the branch of the family who lived on Dewees Island comes from two sources: vital statistics recording births, marriages and deaths, and legal documents reporting real estate transactions and court proceedings. Researchers have not found any diary or memoir, and there do not appear to be any surviving letters or memoranda by a family member that would provide information. Consequently, any attempt to describe the life of the Dewees family in America will leave many gaps. Some of these may be filled by conjecture; others simply remain a mystery.

In the mid-1660s, Garrett Hendricks Dewees, together with his family, left his native Netherlands and settled in the American colonies. His destination was not the Carolinas; several more years were to pass before the founding of Charles Town. Garrett Dewees may have lived for a time in New York, for three of his children were baptized there, but the family's eventual destination was Germantown, Pennsylvania, now a part of Philadelphia. Germantown began as a community of German-speaking immigrants and the Dewees family found a home there.

Garrett Dewees and his wife Sjitske had nine children. The sixth child, Willem, was born about 1679, married Anna Christina Mehls and lived in Germantown until his death in 1745. Willem and Anna also had nine children, all of whom lived until adulthood. Most of the children lived and died in or near Germantown. The lives of the two youngest sons, Cornelius and Philip, took a different course. Cornelius was born in 1719, almost certainly in Germantown, and married Phillipina Boehm about 1748. Their four children, William, Mary, Sarah and John, were born between 1749 and 1755, all of them probably in Gloucester County, New Jersey. Philip was born in Germantown about 1721 and married Elizabeth (whose last name remains unknown). They had one child, Andrew, who was born about 1753.

At least by 1759, and probably several years earlier, both Cornelius and Philip were living in Gloucester County, New Jersey, across the Delaware River from Philadelphia. Two years later they were in Charles Town. There is not any written report explaining this move, but court records in Gloucester County provide a clue. A civil suit brought against Cornelius by Kezia Falman in 1759 found him liable for damages in the amount of three thousand pounds, a sum roughly equal to $250,000 in today's dollars. At the same time, Philip was defending a claim by Joseph Wood in a suit that apparently never came to judgment. The Dewees Family Association newsletter suggests that these legal problems motivated Cornelius and Philip to leave New Jersey.

There are few hints as to the reason the men selected Charles Town as a new residence. It is known that ships built in coastal Carolina enjoyed an outstanding reputation for strength and durability. Live oak timbers were used for hulls and pine for decking. Cornelius may have commenced building ships soon after his arrival in Charles Town. It is conceivable that he had gained shipbuilding experience in New Jersey that he could employ on a South Carolina island.

No record has been found of the date Cornelius Dewees acquired the island known as Timicau or who was the immediate previous owner. It is probable that by the late 1760s Cornelius was operating a shipyard on the island, one of three in the Charles Town region. The South Carolina *Gazette* of August 18, 1771, carried a news item regarding local shipbuilding beginning with the statement: "There has been built lately, and launched here, a fine brigantine at Mr. Cornelius Dewies's Island." This was the *Neptune*, a model of which Tom Boozer constructed and presented to Dewees Island.

The *Gazette* item is the principal evidence that Cornelius Dewees's occupation was shipbuilding. Another possibility is that Dewees was primarily a planter. Either before or during the time that Cornelius Dewees owned the island a plantation was built. It consisted of a comfortable dwelling house of five rooms, an overseer's house, a barn, cornhouse, kitchen, stable, poultry house, dairy, smokehouse and cabins for up to thirty slaves. This description indicates that agriculture was economically important, perhaps even more important than shipbuilding. When Cornelius Dewees signed a legal document in 1775, he was identified as a planter. When the island was offered for sale in 1791 no mention was made of a shipyard, but an advertisement of the island claimed that four hundred acres were good for indigo, rice and cotton. Much later an article in the Charleston *Evening Post* asserted that these crops made the original owners wealthy. When Dewees Island was sold in 1925, it was reported that "there are still signs of levees and dikes which separated the rice and cotton fields in olden times."

Cornelius's wife died in 1769, and the following year he married a widow, Sarah Minor. They were to have three daughters, Margaret, Ann and Rebecca. Besides Cornelius's ownership of the island, he also owned a house on Meeting Street in Charles Town. It is probable that, along with other prosperous Charles Town residents, Cornelius lived at least part of the year in his city home.

In addition to the shipyard and plantation, Cornelius Dewees was active in the purchase and sale of real estate. Apart from the Meeting Street house and lot, Cornelius owned at various times Charles Town lots on Pinckney Street, Wragg Street and Colleton Square, half of Capers Island and tracts in Berkeley and Craven Counties and on the Saluda River.

All of this indicates that by the mid-1770s Cornelius Dewees enjoyed financial success. He also continued to have legal disputes, one of which required him to convey conditional ownership of Dewees Island to John Savage in order to secure payment of a financial obligation. In some way that obligation was compromised (although not fully satisfied), for Cornelius Dewees regained ownership. Incidentally, the Renunciation of Dower, which Sarah Dewees executed in order to permit the conditional sale to John Savage, is the earliest reference to the island's modern name. Sarah agreed to the sale of "all that his the said Cornelius Dewees' Island or Plantation anciently known by the name of Timicau, now Dewees Island."

Considerably less is known about Philip Dewees's residence and business in Charles Town. Although he must have moved to South Carolina at about the same time as Cornelius, he does not appear to have had any connection with the shipyard. He lived in Charles Town and is remembered as a merchant.

The Hunting Islands in the American Revolution

It is sometimes thought that the American Revolution began with the Declaration of Independence, with somewhat earlier hostilities at Lexington and Concord. In South Carolina the Revolution began at least as early as it did in Massachusetts. In 1775 a state of war existed between England and the colony. In the spring of that year there was a break-in at the Charles Town armory and the theft of eight hundred rifles and sixteen hundred pounds of powder. The thieves were never apprehended, largely because they were prominent Charles Town citizens. Later the same year, rebels seized Fort Johnson, the only fortification bordering the harbor. A committee of safety displaced the colonial government, and John Rutledge became the governor. British loyalists were harassed and many left the city, followed by the royal governor, Lord Campbell, who took refuge on a British warship in the harbor. Campbell asserted that only a few rebels controlled Charles Town and urged British reprisal: "Charles Town is the fountainhead from which all violence flows. Stop *that*… and the rebellion in this part of the continent will, I trust, soon be at an end."

London responded to Lord Campbell's request by directing that a fleet be dispatched to discipline the Carolinas. Ships and troops from Britain would join with vessels already in New York and Boston. Governor Rutledge learned of this plan late in 1775, and ordered Colonel William Moultrie to begin construction of a fort on Sullivan's Island. Fort Johnson could protect the southern part of Charles Town Harbor, but the northern entrance, past Sullivan's Island and Mount Pleasant, was undefended. Moultrie judged that, considering the military urgency, the best defense would be a fort with walls of palmetto logs. Sullivan's Island lacked significant numbers of palmettos, and Moultrie turned to another source. Henry Savage's book, *River of the Carolinas: The Santee*, reports Moultrie's action:

> *Accordingly, in January, Mr. Dewees, who owned the sea island above Long Island, was instructed to furnish palmetto logs until further orders, "not less than ten inches diameter in the middle. One third are to be eighteen feet long, and the other two-thirds twenty feet long." He was to "be allowed one shilling per foot for all such logs as delivered in which delivery the utmost expedition must be used."*
>
> *Of these logs and the sand of the island, with the help of a few other timbers and some iron bolts, the fort on Sullivan's Island was built. The site chosen for the structure was the narrow southwest end of the island, where a wide shallow cove separated the island from the mainland… The design of the fort was simple indeed, a plain rectangular structure… The strength of the work was to be in the double walls, sixteen feet apart, built of Dewees's palmetto logs securely bolted together, with the space between filled with sand. Inside, ten feet from the top, the gun platforms were to be built of heavy oak timber.*

Cornelius Dewees and laborers on Dewees Island began work immediately, cutting and lashing palmetto logs, which were floated to Sullivan's Island and put in place at the fort. South Carolina's flag today displays a palmetto, and so pays tribute to the island that supplied the logs.

Fortunately for the colonial rebels, the British fleet did not reach the Carolinas until May 1776. It was delayed first by difficulty in recruiting soldiers, and then by storms that separated the fleet. Eventually a force of fifty vessels and three thousand British soldiers reached the mouth of the Cape Fear River. There they learned that loyalists marching from upland North Carolina had been defeated and scattered at Moore's Creek Bridge. Upon receiving this report, Admiral Peter Parker and General Sir Henry Clinton selected Charles Town as their destination. On May 31, lookouts on Dewees Island observed the British fleet off the island and at once notified Governor Rutledge. Colonel Moultrie prepared for battle and dispatched Colonel William Thomsen and six hundred riflemen to the north end of Sullivan's Island. Four hundred defenders remained at the fort with sixty-two guns to oppose warships armed with more than two hundred guns.

Parker anchored his fleet off Dewees Island, while he and Clinton determined strategy. They decided to coordinate an infantry attack from the north of Sullivan's Island with a bombardment by sea. Clinton's understanding was that Breach Inlet separating Long and Sullivan's Islands was only two or three feet deep and easily forded. On June 8, Clinton, without opposition, began landing troops on Long Island. Two thousand eventually came ashore and began a march south to the inlet. It was a difficult and uncomfortable march in June heat through snake-infested marsh, and "moschetoes, than which no torment can be greater." On June 18, Clinton's force reached Breach Inlet and found the water depth to be eight to nine feet even at low tide. Swift currents made crossing on foot impossible. Clinton had only a few landing boats and every attempt to cross by water was repulsed by Thomsen's riflemen. As a consequence, landing on Sullivan's Island was abandoned. An English newspaper reported the incident with a poem titled "A Miracle on Sullivan's Island":

> *By the Red Sea the Hebrew host detained*
> *Through aid divine the distant shore soon gained*
> *The water fled, the deep a passage gave*
> *But thus God wrought a chosen race to save.*
> *Though Clinton's troops have shared a different fate*
> *'Gainst them, poor man! Not chosen sure of heaven*
> *The miracle reversed is still as great—*
> *From two feet deep the water rose to seven.*

Admiral Parker reasoned that his ships could destroy the Sullivan's Island fort even without land support, and when weather permitted he crossed the bar into Charles Town Harbor. On June 28 he anchored nine ships, including two carrying fifty guns each, and commenced shelling the fort. The fort's palmetto logs did not shatter; the cannonballs did not penetrate the fibrous wood. Moultrie's forces were short of ammunition. During the day they ceased firing for a time to conserve powder, but their guns caused great damage to the two largest warships and the loss of each ship's captain. Three other warships attempted to round the tip of Sullivan's Island and open fire from behind the fort. They went aground on the shoal where Fort Sumter would later be constructed.

Two vessels floated free as the tide rose, but the third was destroyed by the firing from the fort. As night came on, the British fleet withdrew from Charles Town Harbor and made no effort to renew the battle.

After the engagement the fleet returned to waters off Dewees Island to rejoin transports carrying Clinton's troops. One transport ship, the *Glasgow*, armed with six four-pounder guns, provided cover for the other vessels but went aground trying to sail from Dewees Inlet. Before a rescue party could return, men from a ten-gun row galley from Dewees Island boarded the *Glasgow*, captured its crew and fifty Highlanders on the ship, removed all that could be taken and set the *Glasgow* on fire. The American gunboat was manned by a crew from Dewees Island, including Cornelius Dewees and his son William.

As the American Revolution continued, Dewees Island was called on to supply more wood for Fort Moultrie. In January 1780 Colonel Charles Cotesworth Pinckney wrote the fort's commander, Isaac Harleston, directing him to send soldiers "to Dewees's Island to serve as a covering party there to the Negroes who are to cut wood for the Garrison." This was firewood rather than palmetto logs.

Charles Town was spared attack for two years following the battle on Sullivan's Island, but in 1778 the British sent another force to the Southern colonies. It captured Savannah and moved into South Carolina. In 1780 the British army reached Charles Town and after a siege of several months the city surrendered and was occupied for the duration of the war. In December 1781 the British commandant of Charles Town banished wives and other dependents of rebels who would not swear loyalty to Britain. The Continental Congress voted a payment of $30,000 to support dependents who had traveled to Philadelphia. Cornelius Dewees's wife, Sarah, was a named refugee. In 1782, the commandant issued a list of persons regarded as disloyal to the Crown. These persons were ordered immediately to leave Charles Town. Cornelius's son William was on the list. Cornelius Dewees himself was not named as an exile or deportee. In view of his service to the revolutionaries, he could hardly have remained on Dewees Island. Perhaps he joined Francis Marion in the Santee swamps. He did survive the war and returned to the island.

Departure of the Dewees Family

The British occupation of Charles Town and its adoption of measures to punish and control the rebellious colonists did not bring order or submission. Guerilla warfare continued in the countryside outside Charles Town, and the British retaliated by burning churches and homes and destroying crops. There is no record of what may have occurred on Dewees Island. When the island was offered for sale in 1791, there was not any mention of a shipyard. It seems at least possible that the shipbuilding structures were destroyed after the British capture of Sullivan's Island and Mount Pleasant. The Dewees plantation house, however, was not destroyed.

In December 1782 the last British troops left Charles Town. The orders of banishment were revoked, and exiles returned to their homes or to the ashes of burned houses. The

Dewees family was reunited. Philip Dewees had died in 1778, but his son Andrew was in Charles Town. Both Cornelius and Sarah returned, and their sons William and John. The daughters had married and generally settled in or near Charles Town.

But for the Dewees family, life could never again be the same. They had gone through a harrowing war, separated from one another, Sarah a refugee probably in Philadelphia, William an exile threatened with death or imprisonment if he returned and Cornelius a fugitive with no record of his whereabouts. Dewees Island had also changed. The shipyard was gone, never to be restored, and the island land was used for pasture and farming. In the years after 1782, Cornelius transferred to family members much of the property he had acquired. His part-ownership of Capers Island went to William, who sold to Gabriel Capers. The house on Meeting Street in downtown Charleston was given to John. (At the conclusion of the Revolutionary War in 1783, South Carolina changed the city's name from "Charles Town" to "Charleston.") In 1790 John died, probably in Charleston. Philip's son Andrew became a wealthy planter in Charleston and owner of thirty-four slaves. He left the city in 1791, having received a Spanish land grant, and resided in east Florida until his death in 1794. William Dewees lived in Charleston after the Revolution and prospered as a merchant. He owned a wharf running from East Bay Street to the Cooper River at the foot of Queen Street. He died in Charleston in 1827, and his obituary took pains to record that he overcame poverty in his youth to gain wealth and prominence, a rather surprising statement in view of Cornelius Dewees's shipbuilding and real estate undertakings.

Cornelius himself died in 1786 "at his plantation." William and John were named as coexecutors of his estate. He was survived by Sarah, who later remarried and moved to Barnwell County, South Carolina.

The ownership transfer of Dewees Island followed a complicated and confusing course. In 1775 Cornelius and Sarah Dewees had executed a conveyance of the island to John Savage as security for a debt owed by Cornelius. Savage was the first president of the Charleston Chamber of Commerce, a wealthy merchant and partner of Gabriel Manigault. Savage had opposed the boycott of tea imported from England. In some manner the debt was resolved and ownership of the island reverted to Cornelius. Subsequently Cornelius and Sarah conveyed ownership to their nephew, Andrew Dewees. The reason for this is not known. Cornelius and Andrew had not been especially close and were separated during the war years. Andrew was not an executor of Cornelius's will and never showed an interest in residing on the island. Probably a commercial or legal consideration was involved, perhaps dating back to Cornelius's dealings with John Savage. The possibility of a connection with John Savage is supported by a "mortgage in fee" concluded in 1784 by Andrew and Catherine Dewees with William Phillips. This document recited that Andrew was indebted to George Smith and Samuel Legare "for the use of John Savage late of Charleston," and that at Andrew's request William Phillips had cosigned the indebtedness. To secure Andrew's obligation he conveyed Dewees Island to Phillips, with the proviso that if Andrew should pay Messrs. Smith and Legare the full amount of the obligation with interest and indemnify Phillips against any claim arising from the transaction, the conveyance would be void.

What is known is that in 1791 the *City Gazette and Advertiser* published an advertisement for the sale of Dewees Island. After describing the island's virtues, the advertisement concluded: "It is unnecessary to say anything of the air of this beautiful spot as the benefits arising from it have been experienced by numbers, who from a declining state have been restored to perfect health." The notice was placed by George Smith and Samuel Legare, along with Messrs. Desaussure and Darrell. No report has been found of the results of the advertisement, but there is some evidence that the purchaser was Daniel Desaussure.

Post-Revolution Tensions

A peace treaty in 1783 acknowledged the independence of the United States of America, but it did not resolve the disputes between Great Britain and its former colony. The whole matter of commerce between the nations was unsettled, and there were sharp disputes concerning the unexplored lands to the west. Potential for hostilities grew more severe when England and France went to war in 1792. As hostilities increased, President Washington urged upon his countrymen a policy of noninvolvement in the affairs of Europe. Conflict in Europe, however, was bound to involve the United States. Commerce to Europe was vital to the American nation. At least in matters of trade, the United States could not and did not abandon shipments of domestic products.

England and France each prohibited the shipment of cargo to the other and confiscated ships seized on the high seas bearing goods destined for the enemy. The United States proclaimed a doctrine of freedom of the seas, an assertion denied by both France and Great Britain. Britain with its dominant navy was in a stronger position to interdict shipment to France, but each country halted and searched United States merchant ships and confiscated both cargo and vessels engaged in forbidden commerce. To this end each entered United States coastal waters. One of the incidents of this action occurred off the coast of Dewees Island.

Robert Cochran owned a shipyard in Charleston and was also a captain in the United States Navy. In the summer of 1798 he was in command of the revenue cutter, *Unanimity*, patrolling the South Carolina coast north of Charleston in search of French vessels threatening American ships. Off the coast of Dewees Island he sighted a ship that he identified as a French privateer. (It seems to have been the practice at that time for ships not to fly a national flag, and on occasion even to fly an enemy's flag if that would deceive a foe.) Cochran opened fire on the other ship, which returned the shooting. Neither vessel seems to have damaged the other. After the opening action, Cochran fled for safety to Dewees Island, but struck the bar at the entrance of Dewees Inlet, going fully aground. The other vessel approached and after learning the nationality of Cochran's ship, identified itself as the HMS *Mosquito*, an English ship also engaged in apprehending French privateers. A report of the battle of Dewees Inlet reached United States Naval authorities, who dismissed Cochran for cowardice. He returned to the operation of his shipyard, undaunted by his experience in combat.

Chapter 6

The Lost Century

The southern landscape of 1880 bore the signs of the preceding twenty years. Symmetrical rows of slave cabins had been knocked into a jumble of tenant shacks. Fields grew wild because it did not pay to farm them. Children came upon bones and rusting weapons when they played in the woods. Former slave owners and their sons decided which tenants would farm the best land and which tenants would have to move on. Confederate veterans at the court house or the general store bore empty sleeves and blank stares. Black people bitterly recalled the broken promise of land from the Yankees and broken promises of help from their former masters and mistresses. Everyone labored under the burdens of the depression that had hobbled the 1870s. Men talked of the bloodshed that had brought Reconstruction to an end a few years before.
— *Edward L. Ayers, The Promise of the New South, 1992*

This quotation and others like it describe conditions in the rural South after the Civil War. We can be quite sure that they apply to Dewees and other barrier islands. But generalities do not provide specifics of life on Dewees, and unfortunately there are only a few firsthand descriptions of what happened on Dewees Island during those years. For that matter, there are few reports of what happened on Dewees Island during most of the nineteenth century. There do not seem to have been surviving letters, diaries or memoirs that could tell us the experience of real people. The lack of contemporary information provides the title of this chapter: The Lost Century.

It seems certain that after 1800 farming was the principal economic activity on Dewees Island. Shipbuilding did not resume after the Revolutionary War. There were great quantities of oyster shells on the island, mostly in mounds dating back to Sewee Indian times, and these were used for the production of lime. Live oaks and palmettos probably were cut and sold. There is not any record of other nonagricultural activity. The owners of Dewees Island in the nineteenth century were commonly identified on census records as farmers or oystermen, with an occasional carpenter. In 1800 only one hundred acres of land on Dewees Island had been cleared, and a substantial part of that was range for livestock. It is not possible to judge accurately whether Dewees residents prospered in the years before the Civil War.

Identification of the nineteenth-century owners and residents of Dewees Island comes principally from a short historical outline written by Anne King Gregorie, probably in the 1930s, and from ongoing historical research by Linda Dayhoff Smith. Dr. Gregorie was a resident of Mount Pleasant and a South Carolina historian, but the history of Dewees was written for the entertainment and edification of her friends on Dewees Island. Mrs. Smith's search through records at the South Carolina Department of Archives and History has contributed significantly to my understanding of life on Dewees Island and the people who lived there.

In 1796 Elizabeth, the wife of John Thompson Deleisseline, desired to invest an inheritance by purchase of Dewees Island. As was then customary for a married woman with property, trustees were appointed to make the purchase. One of the trustees refused to serve, and the other, John Lewis Poyas, acted as sole trustee. Poyas, a resident of Daniel Island, purchased Dewees Island from Daniel Desaussure, transferring part of it to Elizabeth in his capacity as trustee and retaining the remainder in his name. In 1800 Poyas and Mr. and Mrs. Deleisseline presented claims against each other disputing whose money had been used to purchase the island and who was entitled to the income from the sale of palmetto logs. Neither a published outcome of the suit nor deeds describing the respective parcels of land have been found.

In 1804 there was a recorded partitioning of the island. Poyas received three hundred acres to the north and Mrs. Deleisseline 279 acres to the south, including the plantation house of Cornelius Dewees. This land division continued until 1898. The total island acreage involved in the partition was described as 579 acres. This was a good deal less than the island's size, but it may be that marshes were not included. They could not be used in the island's economic life. It also appears that Lavender Point at the extreme north end of the island was not included.

The exact location of the Dewees house has never been settled. It was probably on the south or southeast part of the island, fronting on Dewees Inlet. As late as the Huyler ownership of Dewees Island, the road named Dewees Inlet Drive was known as "slave street," a clear indication that the slave cabins mentioned in 1791 lay along it.

The uneasy peace between the United States and Great Britain ended with the War of 1812. There is no family record of what the Dewees Island owners did after the outbreak of war. Probably they moved to the comparative safety of Charleston.

In August 1813 British ships cruising off the coast conducted several raids on Dewees and Capers Islands. On the earliest occasion they entered Dewees Inlet and destroyed two boats belonging to Elizabeth Deleisseline. The following day a schooner was captured and burned. Three days later British forces landed on both Dewees and Capers Islands. They burned some small boats and also carried off livestock and provisions. Houses on both islands were plundered. There were not any defenses on either island, and no resistance was made to the invaders.

Between the War of 1812 and the Civil War, we have only isolated stories of Dewees owners and events. In the 1820s a tragedy took place on the Deleisseline plantation. An

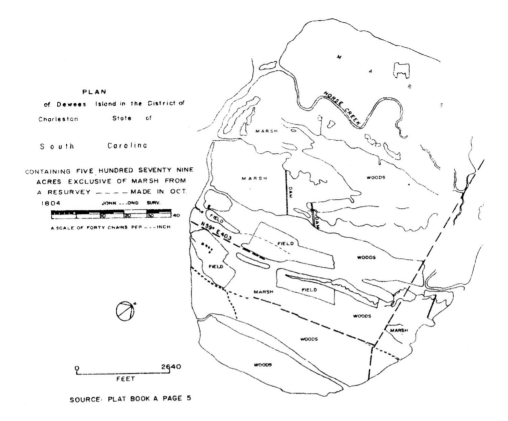

PLAN

of Dewees Island in the District of

Charleston   State   of

S o u t h   Carolina

CONTAINING FIVE HUNDRED SEVENTY NINE
ACRES EXCLUSIVE OF MARSH FROM
A RESURVEY _ _ _ _ MADE IN OCT.
1804   JOHN ...OND SURV.

A SCALE OF FORTY CHAINS PER _ _ _ INCH

0   2640
FEET

SOURCE: PLAT BOOK A PAGE 5

Map of partition of Dewees Island, 1804. *South Carolina Department of Archives and History.*

outlaw from Charleston, fleeing from arrest, reached Dewees Island and hid there. The pursuing officer appealed to young Thomas Deleisseline to assist in finding the fugitive. It is not clear whether Thomas was in residence or came from the mainland. He opened the door of his house and was fatally shot by the outlaw. A posse pursued and shot the fugitive on the mainland.

In 1823, upon petition of the heirs of John Thompson Deleisseline, his portion of Dewees Island was sold at auction to his son John. Some years later John Deleisseline appealed from an order directing him to furnish slave labor to work on public roads. He protested that it was difficult to transport laborers across open water and that in the previous winter two slaves had frozen to death when the boat carrying them went aground. His appeal however was denied. John Deleisseline died at his Dewees home on January 14, 1840, and was buried in Mount Pleasant at the cemetery of old Christ Church. His widow inherited all his property, including the island, but with the proviso that she should leave Dewees Island to "either of my surviving relations she may think deserving to receive it." But the widow, Rebecca Elizabeth Rivers Deleisseline, later married Leonard Haseldon and upon her death she left Dewees Island to Haseldon in her will. This brought on a family dispute between Haseldon and the Deleisseline heirs. A. Foster Black, a merchant in Charleston, was appointed administrator of the property. Some time later Lucius B. Northrop, a Charleston attorney, succeeded Black. (These transactions took place immediately before or during the Civil War, and many records for that period were lost or destroyed.) In 1868 Northrop sold the land to Edward Jamison Jones for $1,050.

In the years of the Civil War the city of Charleston was under nearly constant siege. A major part of the siege was on land as Union forces bombarded the city and attempted to invade from islands to the south. Another part of the siege was carried out on water through a naval blockade of Charleston. This was resisted by the use of blockade running vessels and attacks on the Yankee ships, climaxing with the sinking of the blockading vessel USS *Housatonic* by the Confederate submarine *H.L. Hunley* off the coast of Sullivan's Island.

A week after the first firing on Fort Sumter, President Lincoln ordered a blockade of South Carolina ports. The economy and military defense of the Confederacy depended upon regular receipt of military supplies and export of cotton, and closing the region's ports could cripple the Confederacy's ability to defend itself. Initially the blockade had little effect. Few United States Naval vessels were available, and those that were assigned to blockade service had limited maneuverability and were too deep in the water to follow blockade runners along the coast. It has been asserted that more than 80 percent of Confederate ships running the blockade escaped capture.

This calculation may be based on the experience of blockade running early in the war. By 1863, the Union had captured many of the Southern ports, releasing blockading vessels to concentrate on stopping commerce into and out of Charleston. Ordinary supplies, such as fuel, shoes and clothing, became scarce, while delivery of rifles and lead ammunition was also threatened.

Before the end of the war and the construction of Charleston's jetties, there were four channels into and out of Charleston Harbor. The principal one was the Main Channel, which skirted Morris Island and entered the harbor from the south. Concentration of Union ships and the emplacement of Union guns on Morris Island made that channel extremely hazardous for Confederate shipping.

An alternate channel from the north became the preferred route for blockade runners entering and leaving Charleston Harbor. The blockade extended as far north as Bull's Bay, but the coast between that location and Charleston was difficult to patrol. The waters adjoining Capers, Dewees and Long Island changed constantly from tides and storms, and only a ship's pilot thoroughly familiar with the coast could navigate them. About three miles offshore from Long Island was a notorious sandbar known as Rattlesnake Shoal (a name still appearing on coastal charts). An incoming blockade runner could steer toward shore immediately north of Rattlesnake Shoal, and then follow the coast hugging the land and breakers south from Dewees Inlet. At Sullivan's Island the passage was known as Maffatt's Channel, and careful handling could bring a ship under the guns of Fort Moultrie and safely into harbor. The many sandbars offshore from Dewees and Long Islands forced most Union vessels to remain in deeper water and minimized their effectiveness as blockaders. Northern ships were usually positioned north and east of Rattlesnake Shoal, where a swift blockade runner could evade them.

The first Union attempt to close Maffatt's Channel took place in January 1862. Twenty ancient ships were sunk in the channel in an effort to block it. The ships sank into the sand and the ocean currents flowed around them. Within a short time blockade runners could ignore this effort at closure.

Sailors on the blockading ships have recorded several episodes of attacks on individual blockade runners. Many of these incidents took place off Dewees Island, since this was the bearing of ships passing north of Rattlesnake Shoal. In May 1862 a steamer was seen passing inside the shoal. A Union pilot boat pursued it and signaled the blockading vessel *Pocahontas* to open fire. The firing was ineffective and the steamer ran toward Breach Inlet and the protecting guns on Sullivan's Island.

Several months later the USS *America*, anchored north of Rattlesnake Shoal off Dewees Inlet, saw a steamer attempting to pass between it and the shoal. The steamer disappeared in the dusk after being fired upon.

The most successful of Union efforts to thwart blockade running was the sinking of the *Georgiana*. This large and fast blockade runner misjudged the location of Rattlesnake Shoal and ran aground off Dewees Inlet. She was carrying $90,000 in cash and three hundred cases of bourbon. While the *Georgiana* crew rowed to safety onshore, Union sailors boarded the ship, removed the money and liquor and set the *Georgiana* on fire. In 1863 and 1864 three other blockade runners struck the wreck and were themselves lost. The historian Milby Burton wrote of a similar incident off Sullivan's Island. There the British-built blockade runner *Presto* struck the wrecked runner *Minho* with such force that a hole was knocked in the bottom and her captain had to beach her. At dawn, Confederate soldiers hurriedly removed cargo while under fire from Union batteries on Morris Island. Later the Federals learned that the cargo was several barrels of liquor. An officer stationed on Morris Island wrote: "The troops on Sullivan's Island got hold of the liquor and had a 'grand drunk,' and it is alleged that 300 men at that time could have taken that island, but unfortunately it was not known until the opportunity had passed."

The climactic event in the Confederacy's efforts to break the blockade was the attack by the *H.L. Hunley*. A Federal sloop of war, the USS *Housatonic* was a part of the fleet stationed off the coast of the Hunting Islands. The *Hunley* entered those waters through Breach Inlet on the night of February 17, 1864, and sank the *Housatonic* four miles off Sullivan's Island.

The long-term military significance of the *Hunley*'s action has been great, but it had little effect upon the outcome of the Civil War. The blockade continued, and use of blockade runners to evade it persisted until Confederate forces evacuated Charleston in February 1865. For the residents of the Hunting Islands, the blockade and its running were the most visible actions of the war. The Federal ships anchored outside the shoals and the darkened swift vessels that passed in the night had a more immediate impact than did the siege of Charleston.

But were there residents of these islands apart from Confederate forces on Sullivan's Island? Probably any civilians departed for Charleston or inland towns. The islands were not safe. Foraging parties from either side came ashore in search of abandoned livestock. Deserters and escaped slaves could take refuge on the islands. There is not any record of destruction of houses on Dewees Island, but Coulter Huyler Jr., writing in 1975, reports that a house on Capers Island was burned. In 1862 a war tax was assessed against George Washington Roberts, owner of a portion of Dewees Island. Roberts was in the Confederate army, and the South Carolina House of Representatives decided that the tax be "stayed" because the land on which the tax was levied was in "the possession of the enemy." Anne King Gregorie, writing of Dewees Island, asserted: "If the island could speak with the tongues of man, it might tell us many a tale of Civil War days and of blockade runners landing at night with goods from Nassau, or of some hard-pressed captain beaching his craft to keep it from falling into the hands of his enemy."

Something more has been recorded of Mount Pleasant, at least toward the closing months of the war. During the war the entire community was ringed by Confederate fortifications. The line of defense extended to the coast at Copahee Sound and crossed to the Wando River. That would have placed guns within range of Long Island and perhaps Dewees Island as well.

In January 1865 General William Sherman's troops entered South Carolina. The army's plan called for an advance to Columbia, but Sherman wished to keep the Confederates from concentrating their defense. One diversion called for a landing at Bull's Bay. On February 12, thirteen ships were taken off blockade duty to act as transports. Shallow water and stormy conditions prevented many of the Federal vessels from entering Bull's Bay, and smaller boats were kept from landing by a Confederate battery and a small force of cavalry. After four days, Federal forces from the transports landed on Bull Island, crossed the water to the mainland and marched inland to the Cooper River. By this time Charleston had been evacuated, Columbia was ablaze and warfare in South Carolina was followed by military occupation and widespread looting.

We do not know when residents of Dewees Island attempted to return or what they found on their arrival. Across the marshes in Christ Church Parish of Mount Pleasant the destruction was widespread. The church itself was wrecked and many of the houses were occupied by black families claiming that their possession had been promised by the occupying army. Family papers and public records had been destroyed, making difficult the proof of title. Dr. Gregorie wrote that "In January 1866 two white families returned to their plantation homes in the parish, but in the chaotic conditions of the time, they were regarded by their friends as foolhardy, for ruin was on every side, and most of the planters preferred to remain in their summer homes in Mount Pleasant." With the passage of time most of the sea island planters did return. President Andrew Johnson directed restoration of confiscated lands to former owners when they had paid their back taxes. In some cases Federal troops were called in to drive off reluctant blacks.

In the years after the war, the ownership of Dewees Island became more and more confused. On some occasions there were foreclosures and repossessions, while island residents sometimes settled without proof of title.

Henrietta Moore, born on Dewees Island in 1902, and her parents. *Courtesy of Linda Dayhoff Smith.*

The most telling description of life on Dewees Island in the 1880s comes from a lawsuit in 1881 brought in the Charleston County Court of Common Pleas by Edward J. Jones against Louisa M. Portwig and others. Soon after the war's end, Dewees Island was owned by two families, the southern portion by Edward Jamison Jones and the northern by George Washington Roberts. Jones and his wife Abigail had a daughter Charlotte, who married Henry Portwig, gave birth to four children and died when the oldest was sixteen. Their father was destitute and three of the grandchildren lived in the Jones's house. Edward Jones occupied his house under a life estate that barred him from selling the property. Jones and his son brought a friendly suit against the grandchildren to determine ownership rights and clear the title. The suit was referred to a master and his findings regarding the Jones property give an insight into the economic plight of the rural Southerners in the years after the war. Real estate appraisers testified that Dewees Island water was good, the air healthful and the soil fertile, but that it did not produce wealth. Jones's principal income, about $200 a year, came from logging trees, mostly palmetto. Only twenty-five acres of land were improved, producing potatoes, corn, beans and peas. Most of this was used to feed the stock, consisting of a mule, a milk cow, other cattle, sheep and swine. The master judged that the land might be worth one or two thousand dollars and concluded that "the value of the place is the man who can work it."

There are no longer any grave markers on Dewees, but at the time the Huylers lived on the island some stones remained. In a letter of November 10, 1975, Coulter Huyler Jr. wrote that if a visitor should walk inland from his house, turn right and cross over

Cistern constructed at Murphy house ca. 1900. *Courtesy of Anne Anderson.*

to the next point at the edge of the marsh, at the tip of the point, there could be found "small stone markers of graves of some long-silent residents of Dewees." No sign of these markers remains.

Both the Jones's land and that of George Washington Roberts to the north passed through several owners' hands before the purchase around 1898 by John Murphy of both properties and of Lavender Point. For the first time since the partition of Dewees Island in 1804, there was a single owner.

Murphy was a contractor in Charleston who had built homes in the city, and was also a Charleston alderman. During his period of ownership, he raised artichokes and pigs on the island, and also cane for chair seats. He apparently intended to manage a substantial farming and shellfish project on Dewees Island. He hired or contracted with Langdon Todd, Lewis Moore, Joseph Milligan and John Cribb to work on the farm, and J.O. Milligan to plant and harvest oysters and clams. Henrietta Moore, the daughter of Lewis and Rosa Mae Moore (and the mother of Doris Legare Dayhoff), was born on Dewees Island in 1902, probably in the house built by John Murphy.

Murphy was the owner of a steam launch, the *Undine*, which he used to visit Dewees and other property he owned on the Cooper River. Murphy's interest in Dewees was substantial enough for him to build a gray house overlooking Dewees Inlet.

It might have been expected that there would be stable ownership of Dewees Island, but John Murphy died intestate leaving a widow and nine children with debts exceeding the value of his property. Dewees Island was sold by order of the probate court to Julius

B. Hyer, as agent for his wife, Charlotte Deleisseline Hyer. Thus, after an interval of more than a century, the island again came into the possession of a Deleisseline.

Dr. Gregorie concludes her history of Dewees Island with a report of the Hyer personal tragedy.

> *It came about in this way. Captain Hyer owned a boat which ran on Wando River from Charleston to Cainhoy, in rivalry with the boat of a Captain Dutart, of the old Huguenot family Dutarque. The rivalry led to bitter feeling, which culminated one evil day in a bloody fight that left dead Captain Dutart and his son. Tried for his life, Julius Hyer was acquitted on a plea of self defense. After the trial, he came to the peace and seclusion of Dewees Island and lived for a time in the Murphy house. Mrs. Hyer joined him, but not for long. On October 3, 1925, she conveyed the island to Coulter Huyler of New York City and Greenwich, Connecticut, whose little son Jack, after an illness of pneumonia, needed a winter in the South.*

Chapter 7

The Huyler Years

The traveler who follows the modern pavement of the ancient "path" from Charleston to Georgetown, may notice about nine miles from the Cooper River Bridge a wide dirt road bearing to the east and marked "Dewees Island-Coulter Huyler." If, in an adventurous mood he follows this road, he will find that it ends after a mile or so in a little hamlet in the tidewater called Porcher's Bluff. Low in the haze of the horizon beyond the salt marshes he will see a blue line of sea islands, with Dewees and Capers, in the stillness of magic solitude, straight before him. Leading out to the channel a thousand feet from the shore is a foot-bridge flanked by a flag staff.

Having come thus far, our traveler will now demand that we take him farther. So we open the box at the base of the flag staff, run up a signal to the breeze, and in a few minutes we see a white motor boat coming. We meet it at the end of the pier, and stepping on board we find shelter from the fresh sea wind, draw warm rugs over our knees, and speed through the dancing water to the enchanted islands ahead. While sea birds dip and cry about us and schools of fish flee from their pursuers, we relax in the freedom of the open, and almost before we know it we are debarking upon the white sands of Dewees.

—Anne King Gregorie, "Dewees Island," probably written in the 1930s

Between 1890 and 1940 so many Northerners bought or built on Southern land that it became known as the second Yankee invasion. Among the arrivals were Coulter Huyler and his family. They purchased both Dewees and Capers Islands in 1924, built a house on Dewees and returned for winter months until 1956. Their experience and descriptions of Dewees are presented in letters written by the elder son, Coulter Huyler Jr., and the recollections of the younger son, Jack Huyler, as recorded in the *Dewees Chronicles* after Jack's visit to Dewees in 1997 and in a recent memoir that he has written.

Coulter Huyler was a candy manufacturer in New York and Connecticut. His heart's desire was to live on a sea island. After a visit to South Carolina in 1924, Huyler purchased Dewees Island for $25,000 and Capers Island for $35,000. At that time the only house on Dewees was that built by John Murphy on Dewees Inlet. The house was uninhabitable, but nevertheless the residence of Mr. and Mrs. Henry Portwig. Mrs. Portwig was the daughter of William M. Jones, an earlier owner. Coulter Huyler Jr. recalled that the house was also the residence of a tribe of wild goats and neither Portwig nor the goats showed any interest in moving after the Huyler purchase. A slightly better preserved house was on Capers Island, and this was the Huylers' residence until a new home was built on Dewees. The family's initial preference for a location was on a small bluff where Old House Creek met Dewees Inlet. They subsequently decided to build on the marsh, partly to increase the distance from the Portwigs and goats, but also to be beside a much larger creek. Their dock was built on the marsh side of the present Landings Building, where a deep creek, now much diminished in size, flowed from Horse Bend Creek.

Construction of the house on Dewees began in 1925, and in November the family, less Father Huyler, descended on Capers Island, where a four-room cottage received a party of eight: Mother Huyler, Coulter Jr., Jack, two "adopted" children, a Russian governess, a Scottish nurse and a young tutor. This house was already occupied by a retired Methodist minister, Arthur Moore, who acted as caretaker and continued to live in the Capers house after the Huylers' arrival.

The Huylers' great interest, of course, was the house under construction on Dewees Island, and we may assume that the family crossed Capers Inlet on a near daily basis. What they found on their first visit was not encouraging. Large stacks of lumber and bricks and the foundation footing were the only visible signs of a new home. The builder had assembled a crew of workers, who lived in tents on Dewees. They were joined by a variety of animals seeking food or recreation, notably a herd of wild cattle wandering at large through the workers' encampment.

After inspecting the work, Mother Huyler announced to the builder that the family intended to occupy its home by early December and that she would direct the construction. This she did with the result that the family did move, despite the lack of walls, complete roof and washing, cooking and plumbing amenities. Coulter Huyler wrote:

> *That first evening in our new house was reasonably pleasant…in spite of the continuing rain, a rising wind, wild cats that roamed the place at will, and the shuffling about of the builders who kept passing by to see what the white folks were doing…It was really quite cozy huddled around the living room fireplace, with rain on all sides, trying not to fall through the living room floor.*

By Christmas the house was substantially complete. It was a rambling one-story building, built on a cement foundation, with a big living room, kitchen, gun room, seven bedrooms, two bathrooms and five brick fireplaces. Father Huyler arrived in time for Christmas festivities, and the family regularly entertained friends and family thereafter.

During the years the Huylers lived on the island, a number of changes were made on Dewees Island, most of them inconspicuous and none threatening the island's sustainability. A dock was completed on the creek, and a trail connected the landing and

Original Huyler House built in 1925. *Courtesy of Jack Huyler.*

Christmas at Huyler home. *Courtesy of Jack Huyler.*

Forest trail in the 1930s. *Courtesy of Jack Huyler.*

Huyler goat cart. Courtesy *of Jack Huyler.*

the house. Other trails were cut through the woods, and a long bridge was built from the house to the inlet, now the impoundment, and across the water to the beach on Dewees Inlet. A mule-pulled cart was used to transport supplies from the dock. After the Cooper River Bridge (Grace Bridge) was completed, visitors to Dewees could park at Porcher's Bluff where a flagpole had been placed, and raising the flag signaled to the Huylers the need for transportation. A well was dug and windmill installed to draw water.

Three other houses were constructed, one near the present Landings Building for Mr. Moore, who had moved from Capers to become the Dewees superintendent and boat captain; another close to the Huylers' house for Edmund and Viola White, the full-time household help; and a small bunkhouse for workers on the island.

During the Huylers' first years on the island, they traveled in their own boat to Charleston for supplies, a round trip of three hours. Their first boat was a deep keel named the *VV*, which Coulter Huyler Jr. remembered as running aground or rolling while crossing Charleston Harbor. One time it ran aground was on Christmas Eve, and part of the night was spent in the channel mud singing Christmas carols. (Both Coulter and Jack mention this incident, but there is a lack of agreement on the length of time they were aground.) A later boat, a converted navy lifeboat called the *Ark* was more stable, but for really heavy duty a barge was hired. On one occasion the barge transported an automobile to the island. Father Huyler did not want motor vehicles on Dewees, but arthritis so limited his walking that he brought an automobile to the island.

Caretaker's house. *Courtesy of Jack Huyler.*

Unfortunately it was driven too close to the surf, where rising water prevented its rescue. Eventually water reached the electric system, which shorted out, and the car began honking and continued until the battery died; it was not rescued from the surf.

From December 1941 until April 1945 the United States was at war with Nazi Germany. During the early months of the war, German submarines caused tremendous damage to American shipping. Submarines operated close to the U.S. East Coast, sinking tankers and other merchant ships. People living along the coast witnessed with horror explosions and fire as ships were torpedoed. In the spring of 1942, German saboteurs landed from submarines on New York's Long Island, and attempts at landing were made on the Maine and Florida coasts. There was a major risk that U-boats would enter secluded inlets at other coastal locations. A German submarine also laid mines near a shipping channel about four miles off the Dewees Island and Isle of Palms coasts.

To meet these threats convoys were used, even to protect ships operating between American ports, and naval vessels patrolled the coast. There were also shore defenses: the installation of additional gun batteries at forts and military posts, the use of nets blocking beach inlets against submarine entry and construction and staffing of observation towers at many coastal locations. A tower on Dewees Island was built by the army and used by coast guard observers. Coast guardsmen also patrolled the beach at Capers Inlet. A communication cable was installed running from Fort Marshall at the north end of Sullivan's Island, under Breach Inlet, across Isle of Palms, Dewees and

Huyler automobile on barge. *Courtesy of Jack Huyler.*

Submarine tower in the 1940s. *Courtesy of Jack Huyler.*

Capers Islands and finally linked with gun batteries on Bull Island. At Fort Marshall two guns were in place capable of shelling Dewees and its adjacent waters.

Fortunately, it was not necessary to fire the guns. The Battle of the Atlantic gradually turned in favor of the Allies and in 1944 the coast guard patrols were discontinued. The coast guard barracks and horse barn have disappeared, although horseshoes are still found in the sand along Capers Inlet, and the observation tower remains a Dewees landmark.

During World War II a group of Boy Scouts frequently visited Dewees Island for weekend camping. After Friday classes they found rides to Porcher's Bluff where a boat was kept. Often they arrived after dark when no light could be seen. There was a prisoner of war camp near Porcher's Bluff that caused concern, particularly after rumors spread that German prisoners had escaped. It was a relief during the crossing to Dewees Island to see the mast light of the coast guard vessel.

During the war the boys became acquainted with the Huylers, and after the coast guard departure they requested Coulter Huyler's permission to take down a barn and

Capers Inlet from top of tower. *Courtesy of Jack Huyler.*

move the lumber ashore. Huyler gave permission on condition that the boys first remove trash left by the coastal patrols. This was an onerous task, but it was accomplished and the wood was removed for building a shelter at Porcher's Bluff. George Grice, one of the scouts, wrote a memoir of the "TJ Boys'" experience on Dewees Island, including the nights they camped in the submarine observation tower and their walks the length of the island. A copy of this memoir is in the Dewees Island Archives.

During and after World War II the Huylers visited Dewees less frequently. Coulter Jr. was in the diplomatic service, while Jack was teaching and managing the family ranch in Wyoming. The senior Huyler died in 1955, and Dewees Island and Capers Island were sold the following year to a group headed by R.S. Reynolds, chief executive of Reynolds Metals Company. The sale price was $70,000 for the two islands. Reynolds purchased the islands as an investment and as a hunting resort.

Chapter 8

Development of Dewees Island

Dewees....Nature At Her Loveliest
Will Developing It Destroy It?
"Dewees," the brochure says, "is nature at her loveliest."
That's a fact, and though some quibble, it'd be hard to refute.
It also is a fact that "Dewees Island is a privately-owned barrier island on the Atlantic
Coast just 350 yards across Dewees Inlet, north of Isle of Palms."
That's another indisputable claim, printed in a brochure put out by the owners of the
island.
But is it a fact, as the brochure states, that Dewees, with only about 560 acres of
highland, can be developed for 150 homesites plus service areas without damaging what
the owners admit is "one of the most beautiful and unique sea islands on the Atlantic
seaboard?"
—*Gardner Miller, Charleston News and Courier, Charleston Evening Post, April 24, 1977*

Between 1956 and 1972 R.S. Reynolds and his associates owned both Dewees and Capers Islands. At the time of their purchase Dewees was the more favored of the two as a game preserve. There was not any lack of wildlife at any time of the year. Deer and turkey were abundant, and wild boar were so numerous that Coulter Huyler and his family had carried guns whenever walking about the island. There were small herds of sheep and cattle and numerous raccoons, squirrels and opossum. Miles of paths and trails crossed Dewees, providing access to ponds and freshwater wetlands. Ducks and shorebirds were plentiful. Most of these attractions were also features of Capers Island, but Dewees had the lodge that Coulter Huyler had built with its seven bedrooms, five fireplaces, two baths, a living room, kitchen and gun room. The dock that the Huylers used for the *Ark* could be reached by visitors' boats at low tide.

The Reynolds group used Dewees Island only as a hunting retreat. If they had any thoughts of commercial development, these were never put on paper. The Reynolds family visited the island, generally in the winter, and did not have as extended a residence as the Huylers. Reynolds employed Oscar Leppert as caretaker, and during much of the time Leppert and his family were the only island residents. His chief and most unpleasant duty was to patrol the island on the lookout for trespassers. Boaters frequently landed on Dewees, and disregarding the "no trespassing" signs, they camped above the high tide mark. Sometimes they left trash or smoldering campfires. On several occasions Leppert found trespassers in the submarine watchtower.

Reynolds's purchase of Dewees and Capers Islands proved to be a profitable investment as well as a recreational retreat. In 1956 he paid $70,000 for both islands. In 1972 he sold them for $2,500,000. Even taking into consideration the inflation between those years, it is apparent that Dewees and Capers were good moneymakers.

In June 1972 Capers Corporation (the name taken by Reynolds and his associates) contracted to sell Capers and Dewees Islands to Wateree Development Company, a corporation organized by Edward Royall, an attorney in Camden, South Carolina. Wateree then transferred its interest to Citizens and Southern National Bank as trustee under the Capers-Dewees Trust, and investors in Wateree took their participation to the Capers-Dewees Trust, and thereafter also to Seewed, Inc., a corporation having the same ownership as the trust that undertook the business management and development of Dewees Island.

The Seewed investors were a group of South Carolina businessmen and professionals, headed by Edward and Robert Royall. All of the participants had had experience with the islands as boaters, fishermen and hunters and knew of their attractions. Some undoubtedly had camped on the beaches and seen the beauty of the sandy shore and the thick maritime forest. Speaking for all, Edward Royall called Dewees Island a paradise that would remain that way.

Before negotiating sale of Dewees and Capers to the Royall group of investors, Reynolds had offered to sell both islands to the State of South Carolina for use as a nature preserve. The asking price was $2,225,000. Governor John C. West recommended the purchase, to be financed by an increase in the state's documentary stamp tax. The legislature refused to approve the tax increase, and the islands were sold to the Royall investors for $2,500,000.

At the time the Royalls and their associates purchased Dewees and Capers Islands, they envisioned using Dewees Island as a hunting and fishing retreat much as Reynolds had used it. It was the recreation and the wildlife on Dewees that attracted them.

The earliest indication that there might be other plans came in 1975. The State of South Carolina, which had declined to pay $2,225,000 for both islands, purchased Capers Island from Seewed for $2,500,000. At the same time and as a part of the sale agreement, all of the Dewees Island owners granted the South Carolina Wildlife and Marine Resources Department a conservation easement on Dewees Island. This easement allowed limited development on Dewees, subject to a master plan to be prepared by the island owners and meeting WMR requirements. No island construction would be permitted prior to WMR approval except for necessary utilities and services. This easement may have been the first conservation easement in South Carolina. It was granted under a new law, which had been enacted in the mid-1970s at the urging of Governor West. Since then the law has been used extensively for creating conservation

Seining in the 1970s. *Courtesy of Henry and Kitty Beard.*

easements. The Dewees Island easement was drawn rather loosely because neither the state nor the Royall group had experience in such matters. The easement did place a limit of 150 on the number of residential lots, and it prohibited any commercial building. These were the state's principal concerns.

In preparation for the sale of lots on Dewees Island, the Seewed investors appointed Edward and Robert Royall as a management team. Even though Dewees Island could be reached only by water, and it was certain that this would continue to be the only access, the Royall group believed that Dewees could be developed for residential use. Other barrier islands had attracted purchasers of homesites despite the absence of automobile access. The costs of purchase and home construction would be high, but high costs fitted into the island's master plan. Seewed proceeded to seek the necessary governmental approvals and conform to practices that would protect the island's environment. As late as September 1976, however, the Royalls informed the Charleston County tax assessor that no sales of land had taken place since the adoption of a conservation easement, and that there were not any sales pending.

Seewed contracted with the engineering firm of E.M. Seabrook Jr. to supervise the construction of public works, and hired John Deas as project manager. By the end of 1977, Seabrook reported that docking facilities were installed, two miles of road finished and that work was proceeding on a reception center, tennis courts and swimming pool, as well as a marina on the Isle of Palms. Creating an island infrastructure from forest and marsh was a massive undertaking. All told, the Royall group spent about $1,000,000 to prepare the island for the sale of individual lots.

Seabrook notified Seewed in September 1978 that its projects had been completed, obligating lot purchasers to pay any balance outstanding for lots each purchaser had under contract. Seewed initially offered eighty-five lots, priced from $50,000 for beachfront to $30,000 for an interior location. By April 1977, purchasers had signed conditional sales contracts for forty-eight lots, in addition to the original Seewed owners. In mid-1978 Seewed issued protective covenants binding on itself and all future purchasers of lots. Many of the covenants related to house location and construction. Only detached single-family dwellings were allowed, not to exceed three stories in height. It was required that all building plans be approved by Seewed before construction began, and they were to be only "first quality construction meeting aesthetic, conservation and safety requirements." Property owners were required to maintain building and grounds in clean and attractive condition. Trees with a diameter of more that six inches could not be removed without prior approval. Water would be supplied through a central system, but sewerage was a responsibility of the individual homeowner and required approval by the appropriate government agency.

The covenants were surprisingly lenient with respect to motor vehicles. One car per family would be approved for use on Dewees Island, and it should be a small vehicle. Motorboats operated on island lakes and lagoons could not be powered by a gas motor exceeding seven horsepower.

The covenants established a homeowner association, to which all lot owners belonged. The purpose of the association was to "preserve the values and amenities of the Dewees Island development" and engage in other activities of mutual benefit to its members. The association would assess an annual maintenance charge to finance the association activities. The covenants provided that for a period of five years Seewed could change any provision at will, and thereafter with the approval of a two-thirds vote of island lots. An organizational meeting of the Dewees Island Homeowners Association was held May 23, 1979.

In 1980 Ed and Bob Royall each commenced construction of a house fronting on Dewees Inlet. Several years later Bobby Kennedy and the Reverends Duncan and Elizabeth Ely also built houses. The sale of lots, however, was disappointingly slow.

In 1984 Seewed entered a conditional contract for sale of Dewees Island to Drake Development Company. In an effort to accomplish that sale, a special meeting of the homeowners association voted to change a provision of the protective covenants limiting house building to single-family residences. The revised provision allowed construction of "cluster villas," which was understood to mean multiple ownership of residences. Despite this concession, sale to Drake fell through.

In the years that followed, Seewed continued its efforts to sell Dewees Island. In June 1987 the South Carolina Wildlife and Marine Resources Commission approved a change in the 1975 conservation easement. The revised easement permitted the sale of three hundred lots for residential use, a 100 percent increase over the 150 lots originally allowed. Newspaper reports of the change made it apparent that the initiative came from the Wild Dunes Development Company. The Wild Dunes Resort had opened on the Isle of Palms several years earlier, with all of the amenities that had proved popular at other sea island resorts: golf courses, carefully tended lawns, flowering shrubs and homes built close to the dune line with unobstructed views of the ocean.

The Wild Dunes proposal for development of Dewees Island did not contemplate a resort identical to that on Isle of Palms. There would not be a bridge to the island and a golf course was not planned. Most of Dewees Island would remain in its natural condition. The Wild Dunes plan started with 285 houses clustered on 237 acres, with tennis courts, a clubhouse and driving range "all in an equestrian setting."

In the summer of 1987 Seewed and Wild Dunes Development Company signed a contract for sale of Dewees Island. By August, Seewed had options to repurchase all seventy lots needed for the sale to Wild Dunes. (Forty-eight of these had been sold by Seewed to individual purchasers and twenty-two were held by Seewed members.) The Wildlife and Marine Resources Commission approval of the changed environmental easement had been recommended by the WRC staff and approved by Chairman William Webster IV without a public hearing.

When it became known that the State Wildlife and Marine Resources Commission had modified the Dewees environmental easement by doubling the number of permitted homes, opponents of the development voiced bitter dissent. Local political leaders, including Carmen Bunch, the mayor of Isle of Palms, and state representative Eugene D. Foxworth of Charleston, immediately opposed the change and were joined by the Sierra Club, the Charleston Natural History Society and the Atlantic Coast Conservation Association. Many residents of Isle of Palms had resisted any development of Dewees from the beginning. They feared that the water near Isle of Palms would become polluted, and they also suspected that easy access to the Dewees Island beaches would end when houses were built along the oceanfront. The Charleston *News and Courier* added to the attack with a series of critical editorials in the summer and fall of 1987. The newspaper pointed out that the original easement had been worded so vaguely that a change in the permitted number of homes could be made without a public hearing and regardless of its effect on neighboring communities. The State Wildlife and Marine Resources Commission acknowledged the change, passing it off as minor and made necessary by changing conditions. Erosion had caused changes in the island's size, possibly making unusable some of the lots covered by the earlier easement. The new easement increased the required setback from high tide. These were not persuasive defenses and the commission's critics charged that Seewed and the Dewees owners had applied pressure to obtain the change. Representative Foxworth pointed out that Webster, chairman of the Wildlife and Marine Resources Commission, had secured a loan commitment from Citizens and Southern National Bank, whose president was Robert Royall. Foxworth challenged the legality of the wildlife commission's action and asked the state attorney general to advise whether all proper legal steps had been taken. In October 1987 Attorney General Travis Medlock advised that changes in an environmental easement required approval by the State Budget and Control Bureau, and this approval had not been obtained.

This advice effectively invalidated the amendment to the conservation easement, which had increased the maximum number of residential lots. The wildlife commission requested that the Dewees Island owners prepare a new development plan. In the spring of 1988 a revised proposal was submitted, providing for a maximum of 148 homes on Dewees Island. This change responded to complaints by environmental groups, but also brought to a close any remaining interest that Wild Dunes had in purchasing the Dewees property. Wild Dunes cancelled its contract, forfeiting the small down payment it had made.

Another possible purchaser and developer of Dewees Island was Patten Corporation. Shortly after cancellation of the Wild Dunes contract, Seewed approached Patten, and in the spring of 1988 a contract was signed. Patten agreed to buy the island subject to successful completion of several engineering projects. Patten would pay for the work, but only if approval was obtained from several government authorities.

One project was to repair dune damage that had occurred eight years earlier when Hurricane David struck the South Carolina coast. It caused only minor damage on Dewees Island, but it broke through the dune line that had separated Lake Timicau from the ocean. Tidal flow thereafter passed through the entire waterway, scouring and widening the channel. The flow of the new waterway caused significant erosion, particularly to the south of its entry into the ocean. In 1984 the owners of Dewees applied to the South Carolina Coastal Council for a permit to create an embankment that would close the breach and restore the island waterway to its former condition. With the inlet closed, new sandbars would be formed in the ocean permitting sand to drift ashore. The coastal council issued a permit conditioned on Seewed's assurance that tidal flow into Velvet Creek and Lake Timicau would not be disturbed, and that water in the lake would continue to be aerated. Before work commenced, suit was brought by a group of fishermen to block construction. The inlet had become a popular fishing spot and opened Dewees Island to increased traffic.

In 1987 Judge David Maring of the Charleston Court of Common Pleas dismissed the suit. He took note that Seewed was the owner of Dewees Island, including that part of the island that had been torn away by Hurricane David. As a property owner, Seewed had the right to reclaim land that had been taken by a hurricane. Judge Maring made it plain that while Seewed had the legal authority to restore the land to its former condition, it did not have the right to change the water conditions.

Patten succeeded in restoring the embankment separating Lake Timicau from the ocean. It was expensive work because of the necessary heavy equipment used and the repairing of damage to roads. Within two weeks after restoration of the embankment, fishermen and shrimpers complained to the South Carolina Coastal Council that 150 acres of marsh and water in Lake Timicau had become stagnant, violating the earlier assurances by Seewed that closing the breach would not disturb tidal flow. Officials from the Wildlife and Marine Resources Commission visited the site and reported that water quality was good. This report was not accepted by the complainants and the issue was still pending in the fall of 1989, when Hurricane Hugo breached the dike again.

Patten's other major concern was the adequacy of the planned wastewater treatment system. Seewed's engineers had designed a system with a septic tank at each outlet followed by parallel gravel tanks. Waste would be pumped from the tanks to mainlines and to a holding tank that distributed to a central wastewater field. Approval by the Department of Health and Environmental Control was essential to development, and DHEC was in no hurry to give its blessing. This delay led Patten to terminate its purchase agreement. Patten withdrew from the contract on April 1, 1989, and the contract deposits were refunded.

During the first week of September 1989 a tropical depression, later to receive the name "Hugo," appeared in the Atlantic Ocean off the coast of Africa. As it moved west it gained strength, becoming a hurricane on September 14 and causing loss of life and extensive damage to Guadeloupe, the Virgin Islands and Puerto Rico. Hurricane watchers forecast that Hugo was heading for the United States, but were uncertain which part of the coast was most seriously threatened. On September 20, a hurricane warning was issued for the entire South Carolina coast, and early the next morning an immediate evacuation was ordered for the barrier islands.

Toward evening of September 21, forecasters suggested that the storm might turn slightly north and avoid Charleston, but suddenly it shifted to a westerly course, and Charleston was directly in its path. When it reached land it brought sustained winds of 135 knots and gusts of 150 knots. A wall of water fifteen to twenty feet high swept over the land in Hugo's path. The barrier islands from Folly Beach north to Pawley's Island were the first land to experience the full force of the hurricane.

There were not any people on Dewees Island when Hugo reached the island. Ed and Bob Royall and Bobby Kennedy went to Dewees as soon as possible after the hurricane passed, and were among the earliest to see the devastation along the waterway and on Dewees.

The Ben Sawyer Bridge over the waterway had been so twisted that one end was in the water and the other pointed toward the sky. Boats from Wild Dunes Marina were ripped from the marina and thrown across the waterway to Goat Island. Insulation from destroyed or damaged houses littered the banks. Docks along the water, including the marina dock and the landing dock on Dewees Island, were destroyed.

One of Bobby Kennedy's most vivid recollections was the appearance of his house on Dewees. That house had been surrounded by pines far taller than the house itself. Due to this forestation, the house had been largely invisible from the water. Now the trees were gone and the house stood exposed like a pyramid in the desert.

Old landing dock, 1970s. *Courtesy of Henry and Kitty Beard.*

Ed Royall wrote that the scene looked as if a bomb had dropped on it. Only one or two pine trees remained standing and half of the oaks were destroyed. All of the leaves and many limbs were torn from the trees still standing. All of the island docks were gone and dikes and embankments had been breached. Power poles between Isle of Palms and Dewees were gone, leaving Dewees without power for many months.

The house the Elys owned at the southern end of the beach had washed away, the caretaker's house was totally destroyed and the hunting lodge that the Huylers built still stood, but was so damaged that it could not be inhabited. Stan Betzold, the caretaker, lived for the following five months in the Bob Royall house, to provide security on the island. The houses of Ed and Bob Royall and of Bobby Kennedy did not experience major damage.

When it became possible to bring heavy construction equipment to Dewees, Seewed began the process of restoration. A part of the work was rebuilding the structures the hurricane had destroyed. These included the ferry landing at the Isle of Palms Marina and on Dewees the landing dock, pool, tennis courts and bathhouse, and repair of the water system and well. Completion of the wastewater project and securing a permit from DHEC were also undertaken. The waste disposal field that had been built in the center of the island survived Hugo without damage.

The more formidable work, and work that had to be done before much of the rebuilding could be completed, was to clean up the tree destruction left by Hugo. Much of Dewees Island had been maritime forest, chiefly longleaf pine that had towered above the ground. Substantially all of the pines were broken or killed by the water that covered the island. Burning the wood seemed the most effective way of clearing, and tree branches and trunks were piled in various locations and set on fire. One fire that had been started on the shore of Lake Timicau burned out of control across all of the northern part of the island to the beach at Capers Inlet. To avoid a repetition, trees that had not been burned were stacked on the beach. They may have assisted formation of dunes that are now covered with wax myrtle and groundsel. Seewed spent approximately a half-million dollars clearing debris and restoring the basic facilities on the island.

Years later Jack Huyler, the younger son of the Dewees Island owner who had built the lodge, visited Dewees. He had not been on the island since Hugo, and he described his impression in a letter to his family:

> *There was not one spot on the entire island—and we covered a great deal of it—which looked as it had before Hurricane Hugo. Examples: The creek up which the boat came to our dock is now no more than 10' wide. Our house, departed without a trace except for the brick wall which Dad had built as a windbreak so that he and Mother could sit comfortably on the porch….*
>
> *Tens of thousands of long leaf pine trees were knocked down by the 15' wall of water which Hugo brought to the island from the ocean side and the 10' wave which swept off the leeward side. Dewees is no longer jungly as it was in the old days as soon as one left the beaches or marshes. Those trees, down and dead, were piled and burned by the management. The only good side to their departure is a great depletion of the tick population, which used to be copious.*

Chapter 9

Building a Community for Preservation

Conservation is a state of harmony between man and nature.
—Aldo Leopold, A Sand County Almanac

E ven before the catastrophe of Hurricane Hugo, Seewed faced serious financial problems. In order to sell Dewees Island to Wild Dunes Development Company or Patten Corporation, Seewed bought back lots it had sold to individual property owners (excepting lots owned by the original investors). Inability to complete the Wild Dunes or Patten sales left Seewed with nearly all the land of Dewees Island, but with a large debt and little cash that would be needed for island improvement and marketing costs.

Hurricane Hugo worsened Seewed's financial condition. Clearing the fallen and dead trees, and restoring the essential buildings and services cost more than $500,000. In addition, Seewed was obligated to reimburse Patten for its costs in restoring the beach embankment at Lake Timicau and for its work on the wastewater disposal system.

Seewed recognized the need for a plan for the island's future. After three failures to consummate a sale to a developer, a search for another purchaser of the whole island appeared futile. Nor was the sale of lots to individual purchasers a promising alternative. Hurricane Hugo had shown how fragile the island was. It would be hard to persuade a prospective purchaser, who had seen what a hurricane can do, to invest in such risky property.

The remaining alternative was to attract venture capital from individuals and companies willing to invest in a small South Carolina barrier island. On Dewees the natural beauty was still undisturbed. Visitors admired its pristine beaches, its woodlands and marsh. Ed Royall had said years earlier that Dewees was a paradise, and as a developer he intended to keep it that way. An unspoiled wildness, "a private island dedicated to environmental preservation," was a true and effective description. It would appeal particularly to the successful professional who valued a sanctuary of peace and rest.

William Savage was a native of Camden, South Carolina, and like the Royalls had visited Dewees Island for decades. He was an early investor in Seewed. Savage lived in Alexandria, Virginia, and had extensive experience in real estate and banking. He recommended engaging John Knott, a highly regarded and creative developer in the Washington area to assess the prospects for Dewees Island.

Savage approached Knott and asked him to take a look at Dewees Island and see what might be done to revitalize the island's development. John Knott agreed to visit, and in 1990 he made his first trip to Dewees Island. Years later he wrote of the experience:

> *It has been ten years since I first encountered Dewees Island...when I first walked through her Maritime forest, experienced the serenity of her unspoiled beach, and smelled the salt air that so defines the Island. My immediate reaction of how to "develop" the land was, of course, to do as little as possible. The incredible power of the raw nature of Dewees and the splendor and diversity of her beauty, uninterrupted panoramas, and chorus of natural sounds was an amenity more dramatic than anything I'd ever encountered; quite frankly, it was one of the most intense emotional and spiritual experiences of my life.*

The beauty of Dewees Island did not answer the question of what development was "as little as possible." Knott was convinced that, as Aldo Leopold had written, true conservation was a harmony of man and nature. But how could this harmony be achieved? Knott considered the relation of Dewees Island to the local community, asked his own engineers to study the island's physical resources and reported his recommendations. Bill Savage's response was, "When can you start?" John Knott was startled. He had undertaken an investigation and was now asked to take over its execution. The challenge and promise of Dewees, however, led him to agree to manage, but only if he was given full and unquestioned authority. The Seewed partners agreed to this condition and to John Knott's program for development. This program involved the sale of lots subject to stringent building conditions, and the environmental protection of common property. Charleston real estate and development leaders asserted that prospective purchasers would never accept drastic limits on their freedom. Knott insisted that, on the contrary, purchasers would welcome controls when knowing that all others would be subject to the same controls. Both home values and the natural environment would be protected.

In 1991 Island Preservation Partnership (IPP) was organized with John Knott as its managing director. IPP represented the merging of the Dewees-Capers group and a new investor group brought in by Bill Savage. IPP had the responsibility for developing and marketing Dewees Island, and its authority was exercised through a managing board. Initial members of the board representing the Capers-Dewees Group were Edward M. Royall, Robert V. Royall Jr. and Othniel H. Wienger Jr. Members representing the new investors were William H. Savage, Julian G. Redele and John L. Knott Jr. The Capers-Dewees Trust conveyed to IPP all of Dewees Island exclusive of the land owned by the original investors, while the Investor-Developer Group contributed to IPP money equal to the value of the Capers-Dewees land. IPP assumed all of Seewed's $5,000,000 debt and the personal guarantees given by the Seewed partners. The initial property owners association voted to disband and become part of a new association, consisting of all island property owners. John Knott was named chief executive officer of the reconstituted association.

In May 1996 a new group of investors purchased the IPP interest of Dewees Limited Partners (formerly known as Capers-Dewees Group). Ed and Bob Royall and Othniel Wienger left the IPP Board and were replaced by Guy Paschal, Kimball Whitfield and Anita Zucker. The Charleston *Post and Courier* reported that the purchase price paid by the new investors was $6.1 million.

Early in his tenure as Dewees's chief executive officer, John Knott resolved a long-standing dispute between Dewees management and local environmentalists. At the time of Hurricane Hugo, the South Carolina Department of Health and Environmental Control (DHEC) had not given approval to the proposed wastewater disposal system on Dewees Island. The destructive effects of Hugo postponed further consideration of the permit application until 1990, when public hearings were held. In February 1991 DHEC gave notice that it was approving the permit. An appeal was shortly thereafter filed by the City of Isle of Palms, South Carolina Coastal Conservation League, Isle of Palms Ad Hoc Committee made up of Isle of Palms residents and Atlantic Coast Conservation Association. Their principal spokesman was Dana Beach, president of South Carolina Coastal Conservation League, and a determined advocate of environmental causes. They claimed that discharge from the wastewater system would pollute the surrounding water, endangering human health and destroying marine life. Seewed and the Capers-Dewees Trust denied the charges and hearings were scheduled for the summer of 1991. In advance of the scheduled hearing, John Knott expressed to Dana Beach his belief that the dispute could be settled without further litigation. A meeting took place as John requested. He asked the Beach group what revisions in the wastewater system were needed to minimize hazards to the environment, and his engineers considered these changes with open minds. Agreement was reached, permitting dismissal of the litigation by consent and introducing a new atmosphere of mutual respect and understanding between environmentalists and Dewees management. Carmen Bunch, the former mayor of Isle of Palms, who had contested DHEC approval of the Dewees wastewater system and who had earlier opposed an increase in the number of residential lots, became a supporter of Dewees Island development. Environmental groups did not overtly oppose further development on the island. Orrin Pilkey, an authority on Carolina's barrier islands, who strongly opposed any development on Dewees Island, continued to insist that human habitation on the island was a mistake. He agreed, however, that the Dewees community had made remarkable progress in protecting the island's natural condition.

Within five years after the organization of IPP, Dewees Island was recognized as a leader in green development, resource efficiency, environmental education, waste management and innovative building systems and products. It received awards from South Carolina Land Development, South Carolina Recycling Association, Keep America Beautiful and the South Carolina Wildlife Federation. Subsequently, Dewees Island received the highest award of the Urban Land Institute, and was named by *Coastal Living* magazine as the nation's leading community development.

Dewees Island leadership in conservation and sustainability is apparent in every aspect of island development: public buildings and private homes, educational programs, wildlife protection and management, owner participation and community relations. In

1992 an environmental program was introduced in a temporary nature center, later to relocate to the Landings Building and most recently to the Huyler House. Activities introduced between 1992 and 1994 by the island's first naturalist, Burney Fair, included elementary school environmental studies programs, creation of the schoolchildren's field trip program, organization of the Sweetgrass Basket Program, the production of Dewees Island's first beach sweep and assistance in the creation of the owners' bird counting program. Subsequent naturalists Mark Madden, Arla Jessen and Jonathan Lutz continued and expanded the environmental program Burney Fair had introduced while adding further activities. Mark Madden was a skilled writer who contributed essays to the *Dewees Island Chronicles* and wrote a charming book appealing to all ages, *Discovering Dewees Island*. Mark Madden also introduced the Dewees Discovery Programs, consisting of lectures, discussions and field trips for families to learn more about the island's natural life. Arla Jessen brought in new summer programs, led the Dewees loggerhead turtle nest protection and taught island residents a program for identifying microorganisms in adjacent waters. Jonathan Lutz has enlarged the wet lab under the Huyler House where visitors go "hands-on" with sea creatures and observe tanks of fish, turtles and other wildlife native to Dewees.

The Landings Building itself is a model of environmental landscaping. It is located in a small grove of oak trees, all of which were protected during construction. Other trees were added to shield the building from strong winds and glaring sun. Native plants were added, rainwater was collected in a cistern and the use of pesticides and fertilizers was reduced or eliminated.

The other prominent community building on the island is the Huyler House. Opened in 1998, it presents a classic example of sustainability. The Huyler House has two sections, separated by a breezeway. At one end is a spacious living and dining room, a breakfast room, kitchen and small office now used by the Nature Center. At the other end are four suites, constructed for use by property owners while island houses are under construction, and by prospective lot purchasers who wish to explore Dewees at leisure. Materials from Coulter Huyler's lodge that was destroyed by Hurricane Hugo found a new home in the Huyler House. Window glass tops Huyler House tables, door hardware is displayed and some of the old flooring became a part of the Huyler House floor.

The Huyler House was constructed as a nontoxic and nature friendly building. Its broad porches and windows oriented to catch sea breezes bring the best of outdoor environment to visitors. Guest suites feature nontoxic paints and upholstery of natural fibers. Cleaning products are also nontoxic. The grounds about the house contain plants native to low country Carolina, and a cistern collects and distributes rainwater.

Initially meals were furnished to guests, and frequent dinners were served to island residents as well. It soon became apparent that four suites could not justify meal service. Much of the time the suites were not fully occupied. Food for social gatherings is now furnished by caterers or by the Huyler House users themselves. Property owners who are building homes and prospective land purchasers still use the suites, the annual meeting of the property owners association fills the Huyler House and groups of residents gather for social occasions. Nearly every month there is an artist's reception in the Huyler House, arranged by the Dewees Island Arts Council, and paintings, photographs or sculpture by that artist are displayed. A social committee schedules discussions, concerts and social events, many of which utilize the Huyler House. An island book club meets monthly, and each Wednesday morning the women of the island gather for coffee and to exchange information and ideas.

A third community area on Dewees is the public works. This area includes a public works building housing offices and the reverse osmosis water treatment system. The firehouse, the naturalist's residence, workshops and storage tanks are in this area. There is also a place for vehicle parking, receipt of household waste and a burn area for wood and brush cleared from the island. The wastewater settling field located close to the public works is topped with a grass field on which a helicopter can land when required by medical emergency. The public works is not a candidate for a beautification award, but it serves the basic functions of providing fire protection, emergency services, clean water and proper waste disposal. Dewees Utility Corporation was organized in 1993 to manage the public works. It is responsible for providing island drinking water and disposal of waste. It monitors the wells, tests for purity, removes trash from the island and is a "first responder" to any utility breakdown. The cost of utilities is shared by all property owners, both those living on the island and those who have not yet built.

John Knott's conviction that development and the natural environment are compatible is tested when it comes to house construction. The homeowner has his own ideas about house size and color, building materials, landscaping and dozens of other issues. These may or may not be consistent with the natural appearance and resources of the location where the house will be built. Any planned development must establish some building rules that the homeowner will live with. Dewees Island philosophy requires that those rules be many and demanding for Dewees residents.

An Architectural Resource Board (ARB) was established in 1993. Karl Ohlandt came to Dewees Island that year as landscape ecologist, later to become land manager and advisor to the ARB, and continued in that position until March 2007 when he accepted an appointment as botanist at Spring Island. The ARB adopted guidelines that inform the property owner, his architect and builder of the island requirements. The natural environment shall be minimally disturbed, and "minimally" includes such matters as tree protection and a restricted zone for the builder's equipment and material storage. The house shall be harmonious with the natural landscape. This includes orientation, area, color, siding and roofing. The use of renewable resources is encouraged. Toxic paints and stains are prohibited, as is ozone-destroying insulation. Guidelines require that houses have a minimum impact on neighbors. In all respects, the guidelines first adopted in 1992 remain in effect.

Beach and dune restoration began immediately after Hugo. Grasses were planted, including the treasured sea oat. Sand fences were set out. Beach access was limited to boardwalks crossing the dunes. Storms and currents change the shoreline, and in some years erosion is severe, but the beach is permitted to shape itself. Neither armoring nor artificial sand replacement takes place.

Years before IPP managed the island, the water level in the interior was controlled by spillways in Old House Creek. In 1993 the spillways were replaced with rice trunks

Original Nature Center, ca.1993. *Courtesy of Karl Ohlandt.*

Constructing a boardwalk. *Courtesy of Karl Ohlandt.*

modeled after those used for rice planting. Raising the water level in May and June brings in shrimp, crab and small fish. Lowering the water in the fall and winter maintains water quality and permits waterfowl to locate edible plants.

In the years since Dewees Island was formed, the marsh may have changed less than any other feature. Artificial nourishment of the marsh is not needed or wanted. All the marsh requires is to be left undisturbed. Dewees covenants assure that disturbances will not occur, by prohibiting any house construction close to marshland and restricting approaches to elevated trails that lead to open water.

Freshwater wetlands similarly are protected. Drainage of any wetland is, of course, not allowed. Where cart roads cross wetlands, bridges have been built to avoid disturbing the land. Architectural guidelines specify how close a home may be built to water, marsh or beach dune.

John Knott had three central themes in his philosophy for Dewees Island: harmony of man and nature, sustainability and community. Before he resigned from IPP and POA leadership to direct the Noisette Project, Dewees had progressed far to realize these themes. Through his direction, steady progress was made. After 2000, the property owners of Dewees Island assumed the island's management.

Progress continues. Dewees Island is still a landmark of environmental protection, a working demonstration that man is in nature and can live in harmony with a natural environment. It is now an obligation of the property owners association to carry forward the programs instituted by IPP. Those programs are clear. They require making certain that all who come to the island as owners or visitors understand the Dewees covenants and guidelines, assuring that these covenants and guidelines are enforced fairly and uniformly and encouraging broad participation in island activities. Above all, it must be impressed on all that Dewees Island is a rare treasure requiring cooperation by all. To the extent that this is achieved, Dewees will continue to be a partnership for preservation.

Bibliography

The bibliography is divided into chapters, numbered as are chapters in the book. Some published material deals with topics or time periods discussed in more than one book chapter. To avoid repetition, only the first reference is cited.

Chapter 1

Brewster, Lawrence A. *Summer Migrations and Resorts of South Carolina Low Country Planters.* Durham, NC: Duke University Press, 1947.

Bush, David M., Orrin H. Pilkey Jr., and William J. Neal. *Living by the Rules of the Sea.* Durham, NC: Duke University Press, 1996.

Clarke, Philip G. *Isle of Palms.* Abbeville, SC: Image Graphics, 1998.

Hayes, Jim. *James and Related Sea Islands.* Charleston, SC: Walker, Evans & Cogswell, 1978.

"Impacts of Hurricane Hugo September 20–22, 1989." Articles by various authors. In Special Issue No. 8 of *Journal of Coastal Research* (Spring 1991).

Jordan, Laylon Wayne. *A Place Called St. John's.* Spartanburg, SC: Reprint Co., 1998.

Lennon, Gered, William J. Neal, David M. Bush, Orrin H. Pilkey Jr., Matthew Stutz, and Jane Bullock. *Living with the South Carolina Coast.* Durham, NC: Duke University Press, 1996.

Miles, Suzannah Smith. *A Gazetteer Containing a Concise History of the People, Places, and Events in the Area Known as East of the Cooper.* Charleston, SC: The History Press, 2004.

Savage, Henry, Jr. *Lost Heritage.* New York, NY: William Morrow, 1970.

South Carolina Historical and Genealogical Magazine. Various issues. 1909–1965.

Stringer-Robinson, Gretchen. *Time and Tide on Folly Beach, South Carolina.* N.p., 1989.

Wannamaker, W.W., Jr. *Long Island South.* Columbia, SC: State Printing Co., 1975.

Chapter 2

Applied Technology and Management. "Dewees Island Shoreline Assessment and Review of Pending NFIP Legislation." October 1991, revised November 1991. Dewees Island Archives.

Bertness, Mark D. *The Ecology of Atlantic Shorelines*. Sunderland, MA: Sinauer Associates, 1999.

Davis, Richard A. *The Evolving Coast*. New York, NY: Scientific American Library, 1997.

Dean, Cornelia. *Against the Tide*. New York, NY: Columbia University Press, 1999.

Kana, Timothy W. *Beach Erosion in South Carolina*. Charleston: South Carolina Sea Grant Consortium, 1988.

Kaufman, Wallace, and Orrin H. Pilkey Jr. *The Beaches Are Moving*. Durham, NC: Duke University Press, 1983.

Keener-Chavis, Paula, and Leslie Reynolds-Sautter. *Of Sand and Sea: Teachings from the Southeastern Shoreline*. Charleston: South Carolina Sea Grant Consortium, 2000.

Kovacik, Charles F., and John J. Winberry. *South Carolina: A Geography*. Columbia: University of South Carolina Press, 1989.

RPI Coastal Science Engineers. "Shoreline Assessment of Dewees Island, South Carolina." Dewees Island Archives.

Staper, Frank W., Jr. "Coastal Erosion and Deposition in the Dewees Island Region, Charleston County, South Carolina." November 1982. Dewees Island Archives.

Vernberg, John, and Winona B. Vernberg. *The Coastal Zone*. Columbia: University of South Carolina Press, 2001.

Chapter 3

Ballentine, Todd. *Tideland Treasures*. Columbia: University of South Carolina Press, 1991.

Barry, John M. *Natural Vegetation of South Carolina*. Columbia: University of South Carolina Press, 1980.

Catesby, Marc. *The Natural History of Carolina, Florida, and the Bahama Islands*. Chapel Hill: University of North Carolina Press, 1985.

Drayton, John. *View of South Carolina 1802*. Spartanburg, SC: Reprint Co., 1972.

Fishman, Gail. *Journeys through Paradise*. Gainesville: University Press of Florida, 2000.

Hoffman, Butler and Associates with Coastal Consultants. "Seewed…Dewees." September 15, 1975. Dewees Island Archives.

Madden, Mark. *Discovering Dewees Island*. Dewees Island POA, 1995.

Meyer, Peter. *Nature Guide to the Carolina Coast*. Wilmington, NC: Avian Cetacean Press, 1991.

Porcher, Richard D. *Wildflowers of the Carolina Low Country and Lower Peedee*. Columbia: University of South Carolina Press, 1995.

Sanders, Albert E., and William D. Anderson Jr. *Natural History Investigations in South Carolina*. Columbia: University of South Carolina Press, 1999.

Taylor, David. *South Carolina Naturalists: An Anthology*. Columbia: University of South Carolina Press, 1998.

Wayne, Arthur. *Birds of South Carolina*. Charleston, SC: Doggett Printing Co., 1910.

Chapter 4

Cumming, William F. *The Southeast in Early Maps*. Chapel Hill: University of North Carolina Press, 1998.

Edgar, Walter B. *South Carolina: A History*. Columbia: University of South Carolina Press, 1998.

Espershade, Christopher T., Paul E. Brockington Jr., Joseph L. Tippett, and B.G. Southerlin. "Archeological Survey of Dewees Island, Charleston County, South Carolina." October 1987. Dewees Island Archives.

Gregorie, Anne King. *Notes on Sewee Indians and Indian Remains of Christ Church Parish*. Charleston, SC: Charleston Museum, 1925.

Lawson, John. *A Journal of a Thousand Miles Travel among the Indians from South to North Carolina*. Chapel Hill: University of North Carolina Press, 1967.

Ludlum, David M. *Early American Hurricanes*. Boston, MA: American Meteorological Society, 1963.

Salley, Alexander S., Jr. *Narratives of Early Carolina 1650-1708*. New York, NY: Charles Scribner's Sons, 1911.

Silver, Timothy. *A New Face on the Countryside: Indians, Colonials, and Slaves in South Atlantic Forests 1500–1800*. New York, NY: Cambridge University Press, 1990.

Waddell, Gene. *Indians of the South Carolina Low Country 1562–1751*. Columbia: Southern Studies Program, University of South Carolina, 1980.

Waring, Joseph I. *The First Voyage and Settlement at Charles Town 1670–1680*. Columbia: University of South Carolina Press, 1970.

Weir, Robert M. *Colonial South Carolina: A History*. Millwood, NY: KTO Press, 1983.

Chapter 5

Bearss, Edwin C. *The Battle of Sullivan's Island and the Capture of Fort Moultrie*. Washington, DC: National Park Service, 1968.

Coker, P.C. *Charleston Maritime Heritage 1670-1865*. Charleston, SC: Coker Craft Press, 1987.

Fraser, Walter J., Jr. *Patriots, Pistols, and Petticoats: Poor Sinful Charles Town during the American Revolution*. Columbia: University of South Carolina Press, 1993.

Gregorie, Anne King. "Dewees Island." Essay. Dewees Island Archives.

Lipscomb, Terry. *The Carolina Lowcountry April 1775–June 1776*. Columbia: South Carolina Department of Archives and History, 1991.

McCrady, Edward. *The History of South Carolina in the Revolution 1775–1780, Vol.3*. New York, NY: Macmillan, 1901.

Miles, Suzannah Smith. *Writings of the Past*. Mount Pleasant, SC: King's Highway Publications, 1996.

Petit, James Percival. *Freedom's Four Square Miles*. Columbia, SC: R.L. Bryon Co., 1964.

Ramsay, David. *History of South Carolina, Vol. I*. Spartanburg, SC: Reprint Co.,1959.

Rogers, George C., Jr. *Charleston in the Age of the Pinckneys*. Columbia: University of South Carolina Press, 1984.

Savage, Henry, Jr. *River of the Carolinas: The Santee*. Chapel Hill: University of North Carolina Press, 1968.

Smith, Linda Dayhoff. Research information from South Carolina Department of Archives and History, 2007. Dewees Island Archives.

Chapter 6

Ball, Edward. *Slaves in the Family*. New York, NY: Ballantine Books, 2001.

Burton, E. Milby. *The Siege of Charleston 1861–1865*. Columbia: University of South Carolina Press, 1970.

Gregorie, Anne King. *Christ Church 1706–1959*. Charleston, SC: Dalcho Historical Society, 1961.

Marchand, John B. *Charleston Blockade 1861–1865*. Newport, RI: Naval War College Press, 1976.

Petit, James Percival. *South Carolina and the Sea, Vol. II*. Charleston, SC: State Port Authority, 1976.

Chapter 7

Huyler, Coulter D., Jr. to Mrs. Meta Beard. Letter, 1975. Dewees Island Archives.

Huyler, Jack. "Capers and Dewees Islands." Chapter of unpublished memoir, 2007. Dewees Island Archives.

Report of sale of Dewees Island. *Charleston Evening Post*. December 5, 1955.

Chapter 8

Charleston *Evening Post* and Charleston *News and Courier*. Various articles about development of Dewees Island, 1977–1989.

Huyler, Jack to family. E-mail, 1997. Dewees Island Archives.

Interview with Bobby Kennedy by the author. 2007. Tape in Dewees Island Archives.

Royall, Edward to author. Letter, 2007. Dewees Island Archives.

Royall, Edward. Personal files. Dewees Island Archives.

Chapter 9

Charleston *Post and Courier*. Interview with John Knott. January 31, 1992.

Dewees Chronicles 1991–2001. Dewees Island Archives.

"Dewees Island Architectural and Design Guidelines." July 1992. Dewees Island Archives.

Interview with John Knott by the author. 2007. Tape in Dewees Island Archives.

Seltzer, Harrison P. "Dewees Island's Nature Trail System." University of Georgia's School of Environmental Design, Fall 1994. Dewees Island Archives.

About the Author

James Cochrane is a native of Rochester, New York, attended public schools in Rochester and graduated from Amherst College, where he was a member of Phi Beta Kappa. He is a graduate of Yale Law School.

Cochrane practiced law for thirty-five years in New York City, Rochester and Kingsport, Tennessee, principally as a corporate lawyer. He retired from practice in 1985 and subsequently moved with his wife, Jill, to Charleston, South Carolina.

It was as a Charleston resident that he first visited Dewees Island and experienced love at first sight. The Cochranes have been

Author's photo by Joseph McAlhany Jr.

Dewees Island residents since 2000, and their affection for the island continues to grow. Their first impressions were of its natural beauties: the sun settling behind the marsh, leaving a reflection in the water with bands and splashes of red, orange and blue across the sky; ocean waves cresting offshore and rolling up a white sand beach; dirt roads bordered by oaks and pines, with overhanging branches.

Soon the Cochranes became firm friends with other island residents, with whom they regularly share supplies and experiences. As the Cochranes explored the island and talked with their new friends, they became increasingly interested in Dewees Island life in the past. Who lived here and what were their experiences? How and why does Dewees Island differ from other South Carolina coastal islands?

This book, Cochrane's first publicly published work, is his response to this question and an expression of affection for his island home.